CHRISTIAN WORLDVIEW INTEGRATION SERIES

POLITICS *for* Christians

Statecraft as Soulcraft

FRANCIS J. BECKWITH

IVP Academic

An imprint of InterVarsity Press
Downers Grove, Illinois

InterVarsity Press
P.O. Box 1400, Downers Grove, IL 60515-1426
World Wide Web: www.ivpress.com
E-mail: email@ivpress.com

*InterVarsity Press® is the book-publishing division of InterVarsity Christian Fellowship/USA®, a movement of
students and faculty active on campus at hundreds of universities, colleges and schools of nursing in the United States
of America, and a member movement of the International Fellowship of Evangelical Students. For information
about local and regional activities, write Public Relations Dept., InterVarsity Christian Fellowship/USA, 6400
Schroeder Rd., P.O. Box 7895, Madison, WI 53707-7895, or visit the IVCF website at <www.intervarsity.org>.*

All Scripture quotations, unless otherwise indicated, are taken from the New American Standard Bible®,
*copyright 1960, 1962, 1963, 1968, 1971, 1972, 1973, 1975, 1977, 1995 by The Lockman Foundation. Used by
permission.*

Design: Cindy Kiple

ISBN 978-0-8308-2814-2

Printed in the United States of America ∞

Library of Congress Cataloging-in-Publication Data

Beckwith, Francis.
  *Politics for Christians: statecraft as soulcraft / Francis J.
Beckwith.*
      p. cm.—(Christian worldview integration series)
  Includes bibliographical references and index.
  ISBN 978-0-8308-2814-2 (pbk.: alk. paper)
  *1. Christianity and politics.   2. Christians—Political activity.   3.
Church and state.   I. Title.*
  BR115.P7B343 2010
  261.7—dc22

                                                                                2009042076

P	20	19	18	17	16	15	14	13	12	11	10	9	8	7	6	5	4	3	2	1
Y	27	26	25	24	23	22	21	20	19	18	17	16	15	14	13	12	11	10		

To my dear friend Hadley Arkes,
who taught me about first things
and their indispensable role
in shaping a polity and the
character of its people.

CONTENTS

SERIES PREFACE

A CALL TO INTEGRATION AND THE
CHRISTIAN WORLDVIEW INTEGRATION SERIES

Life's short and we're all busy. If you're a college student, you're *really* busy. There's your part-time job (which seems full time), your social life (hopefully) and church. On top of that you're expected to go to class, do some reading, take tests and write papers. Now, while you are minding your own business, you hear about something called "integration," trying to relate your major with your Christianity. Several questions may come to mind: What is integration, anyway? Is it just a fad? Why should I care about it? And even if I do care about it, I don't have a clue as to how to go about doing it. How do I do this? These are good questions, and in this introduction we're going to address them in order. We are passionate about helping you learn about and become good at integrating your Christian convictions with the issues and ideas in your college major or your career.

WHAT IS INTEGRATION?

The word *integrate* means "to form or blend into a whole," "to unite." We humans naturally seek to find the unity that is behind diversity, and in fact coherence is an important mark of rationality. There are two kinds of integration: conceptual and personal. In conceptual integration, *our theological beliefs, especially those derived from careful study of the Bible, are blended and unified with important, reasonable ideas from our profession or college major into a coherent, intellectually satisfying Christian worldview.* As Augustine wisely advised, "We must show our Scriptures not to be in conflict with whatever [our critics] can demonstrate about the nature of things from reliable sources."[1] In personal integration we seek to live a unified life, a life in which we are the same in public as we are in private, a life in which the various aspects of our personality are consistent with each other and conducive to a life of human flourishing as a disciple of Jesus.

The two kinds of integration are deeply intertwined. All things being equal, the more authentic we are, the more integrity we have, the more we should be able to do conceptual integration with fidelity to Jesus and Scripture, and with intellectual honesty. All things being equal, the more conceptual integration we accomplish, the more coherent will be our set of beliefs and the more confidence we will have in the truth of our Christian worldview. In fact, conceptual integration is so important that it is worth thinking some more about why it matters.

SEVEN REASONS WHY INTEGRATION MATTERS

1. *The Bible's teachings are true.* The first justification for integration is pretty obvious but often overlooked. *Christians hold that, when properly interpreted, the teachings of Holy Scripture are true.* This means two things. If the Bible teaches something relevant to an issue in an academic field, the Bible's view on that topic is true and thus provides an incredibly rich resource for doing work in that academic field. It would be irresponsible to set aside an important source of relevant truth in thinking through issues in our field of study or vocation. Further, if it looks like a claim in our field tends to make a biblical claim false, this tension needs to be resolved. Maybe our interpretation of Scripture is mistaken, maybe the Bible is not even talking about the issue, maybe the claim in our field is false. Whatever the case, the Christian's commitment to the truth of Scripture makes integration inevitable.

Adolfo Lopez-Otero, a Stanford engineering professor and a self-described secular humanist, offers advice to thinking Christians who

---

[1]Augustine *De genesi ad litteram* 1.21, cited in Ernan McMullin, "How Should Cosmology Relate to Theology?" in *The Sciences and Theology in the Twentieth Century*, ed. Arthur R. Peacocke (Notre Dame, Ind.: University of Notre Dame Press, 1981), p. 20.

want to have an impact on the world: "When a Christian professor approaches a non-believing faculty member . . . they can expect to face a polite but condescending person [with a belief that they possess] superior metaphysics who can't understand how such an intelligent person [as yourself] still believes in things which have been discredited eons ago."[2] He goes on to say that "[Christian professors] cannot afford to give excuses . . . if they are honest about wanting to open spiritual and truthful dialogue with their non-believing colleagues—that is the price they must pay for having declared themselves Christians."[3] While Lopez-Otero's remarks are directed to Christian professors, his point applies to all thinking Christians: If we claim that our Christian views are true, we need to back that up by interacting with the various ideas that come from different academic disciplines. In short, we must integrate Christianity and our major or vocation.

2. *Our vocation and the holistic character of discipleship demand integration.* As disciples grow, they learn to see, feel, think, desire, believe and behave the way Jesus does in a manner fitting to the kingdom of God and their own station in life. With God's help we seek to live as Jesus would if he were a philosophy professor at Biola University married to Hope and father of Ashley and Allison, or as a political philosopher at Baylor University married to Frankie.

Two important implications flow from the nature of discipleship. For one thing the lordship of Christ is holistic. The religious life is not a special compartment in an otherwise secular life. Rather, the religious life is an entire way of life. To live Christianly is to allow Jesus Christ to be the Lord of every aspect of our life. There is no room for a secular-sacred separation in the life of Jesus' followers. Jesus Christ should be every bit as much at home in our thinking and behavior when we are developing our views in our area of study or work as he is when we are in a small group fellowship.

Further, as disciples of Jesus we do not merely have a job. We have a vocation as a Christian teacher. A job is a means for supporting our-

---

[2]Adolfo Lopez-Otero, "Be Humble, but Daring," *The Real Issue* 16 (September-October 1997): 10.
[3]Ibid., p. 11.

selves and those for whom we are responsible. For the Christian a vocation (from the Latin *vocare*, which means "to call") is an overall calling from God. Harry Blamires correctly draws a distinction between a general and a special vocation:

> The general vocation of all Christians—indeed of all men and women—is the same. We are called to live as children of God, obeying his will in all things. But obedience to God's will must inevitably take many different forms. The wife's mode of obedience is not the same as the nun's; the farmer's is not the same as the priest's. By "special vocation," therefore, we designate God's call to a [person] to serve him in a particular sphere of activity.[4]

As Christians seek to discover and become excellent in their special vocation, they must ask: How would Jesus approach the task of being a history teacher, a chemist, an athletic director, a mathematician? It is not always easy to answer this question, but the vocational demands of discipleship require that we give it our best shot.

Whatever we do, however, it is important that we restore to our culture an image of Jesus Christ as an intelligent, competent person who spoke authoritatively on whatever subject he addressed. The disciples of Jesus agreed with Paul when he said that all the wisdom of the Greeks and Jews was ultimately wrapped up in Jesus himself (Col 2:2-3). For them, Jesus was not merely a Savior from sin; he was the wisest, most intelligent, most attractive person they had ever seen.

In the early centuries of Christianity the church presented Jesus to unbelievers precisely because he was wiser, more virtuous, more intelligent and more attractive in his character than Aristotle, Plato, Moses or anyone else. It has been a part of the church's self-understanding to locate the spiritual life in a broader quest for the good life, that is, a life of wisdom, knowledge, beauty and goodness. So understood, the spiritual life and discipleship to Jesus were seen as the very best way to achieve a life of truth, beauty and goodness. Moreover, the life of discipleship was depicted as the wisest, most reasonable form of life available so that a life of unbelief was taken to be foolish

---

[4]Harry Blamires, *A God Who Acts* (Ann Arbor, Mich.: Servant Books, 1957), p. 67.

and absurd. *Our schools need to recapture and propagate this broader understanding of following Christ if they are to be thoroughly Christian in their approach to education.*

3. *Biblical teaching about the role of the mind in the Christian life and the value of extrabiblical knowledge requires integration.* The Scriptures are clear that God wants us to be like him in every facet of our lives, and he desires commitment from our total being, including our intellectual life. We are told that we change spiritually by having the categories of our minds renewed (Rom 12:1-2), that we are to include an intellectual love for God in our devotion (Mt 22:37-38), and that we are to be prepared to give others a reasonable answer to questions others ask us about why we believe what we believe (1 Pet 3:15). As the great eighteenth-century Christian thinker and spiritual master William Law put it, "Unreasonable and absurd ways of life . . . are truly an offense to God."[5] Learning and developing convictions about the teachings of Scripture are absolutely central to these mandates. However, many of Jesus' followers have failed to see that an aggressive pursuit of knowledge in areas outside the Bible is also relevant to these directives.

God has revealed himself and various truths on a number of topics outside the Bible. As Christians have known throughout our history, common sense, logic and mathematics, along with the arts, humanities, sciences and other areas of study, contain important truths relevant to life in general and to the development of a careful, life-related Christian worldview.

In 1756 John Wesley delivered an address to a gathering of clergy on how to carry out the pastoral ministry with joy and skill. In it Wesley catalogued a number of things familiar to most contemporary believers—the cultivation of a disposition to glorify God and save souls, a knowledge of Scripture, and similar notions. However, at the front of his list Wesley focused on something seldom expressly valued by most pastoral search committees: "Ought not a Minister to have, First, a good understanding, a clear apprehension, a sound judgment, and a

---

[5]William Law, *A Serious Call to a Devout and Holy Life* (1728; reprint, Grand Rapids: Eerdmans, 1966), p. 2.

capacity of reasoning with some closeness?"[6]

Time and again throughout the address Wesley unpacked this remark by admonishing ministers to know what would sound truly odd and almost pagan to the average congregant of today: logic, metaphysics, natural theology, geometry and the ideas of important figures in the history of philosophy. For Wesley study in these areas (especially philosophy and geometry) helped train the mind to think precisely, a habit of incredible value, he asserted, when it comes to thinking as a Christian about theological themes or scriptural texts. According to Wesley the study of extrabiblical information and the writings of unbelievers was of critical value for growth and maturity. As he put it elsewhere, "To imagine none can teach you but those who are themselves saved from sin is a very great and dangerous mistake. Give not place to it for a moment."[7]

Wesley's remarks were not unusual in his time. A century earlier the great Reformed pastor Richard Baxter was faced with lukewarmness in the church and unbelief outside the church. In 1667 he wrote a book to meet this need, and in it he used philosophy, logic and general items of knowledge outside Scripture to argue for the existence of the soul and the life to come. The fact that Baxter turned to philosophy and extrabiblical knowledge instead of small groups or praise hymns is worth pondering. In fact, it is safe to say that throughout much of church history, Scripture and right reason directed at extrabiblical truth were used by disciples of Jesus and prized as twin allies.

In valuing extrabiblical knowledge our brothers and sisters in church history were merely following common sense and Scripture itself. Repeatedly, Scripture acknowledges the wisdom of cultures outside Israel; for example, Egypt (Acts 7:22; cf. Ex 7:11), the Edomites (Jer 49:7), the Phoenicians (Zech 9:2) and many others. The remarkable achievements produced by human wisdom are acknowledged in Job 28:1-11. The wisdom of Solomon is compared to the wisdom of the "people of the east" and Egypt in order to show that Solomon's wisdom surpassed that of

---

[6]John Wesley, "An Address to the Clergy," in *The Works of John Wesley*, 3rd ed. (Grand Rapids: Baker, 1979), p. 481.

[7]John Wesley, *A Plain Account of Christian Perfection* (London: Epworth Press, 1952), p. 87.

people with a longstanding, well-deserved reputation for wisdom (1 Kings 4:29-34). Paul approvingly quotes pagan philosophers (Acts 17:28), and Jude does the same thing with the noncanonical book *The Assumption of Moses* (Jude 9). The book of Proverbs is filled with examples in which knowledge, even moral and spiritual knowledge, can be gained from studying things (ants, for example) in the natural world. Jesus taught that we should know we are to love our enemies, not on the basis of an Old Testament text but from careful reflection on how the sun and rain behave (Mt 5:44-45).

In valuing extrabiblical knowledge our brothers and sisters in church history were also living out scriptural teaching about the value of general revelation. We must never forget that God is the God of creation and general revelation just as he is the God of Scripture and special revelation.

Christians should do everything they can to gain and teach important and relevant knowledge in their areas of expertise. *At the level appropriate to our station in life, Christians are called to be Christian intellectuals, at home in the world of ideas.*

4. *Neglect of integration results in a costly division between secular and sacred.* While few would actually put it in these terms, faith is now understood as a blind act of will, a sort of decision to believe something that is either independent of reason or makes up for the paltry lack of evidence for what one is trying to believe. By contrast, the Bible presents faith as a power or skill to act in accordance with the nature of the kingdom of God, a trust in what we have reason to believe is true. Understood in this way, we see that faith is built on reason and knowledge. We should have good reasons for thinking that Christianity is true before we completely dedicate ourselves to it. We should have solid evidence that our understanding of a biblical passage is correct before we go on to apply it. We bring knowledge claims from Scripture and theology to the task of integration; we do not employ mere beliefs or faith postulates.

Unfortunately, our contemporary understanding of faith and reason treats them as polar opposites. A few years ago I (J. P.) went to New York to conduct a series of evangelistic messages for a church. The series was in a high school gym and several believers and unbelievers came each night. The first evening I gave arguments for the existence of God from science and philosophy. Before closing in prayer, I entertained several questions from the audience. One woman (who was a Christian) complained about my talk, charging that if I "proved" the existence of God, I would leave no room for faith. I responded by saying that if she were right, then we should pray that currently available evidence for God would evaporate and be refuted so there would be even more room for faith! Obviously, her view of faith utterly detached it from reason.

If faith and reason are deeply connected, then students and teachers need to explore their entire intellectual life in light of the Word of God. But if faith and reason are polar opposites, then the subject matter of our study or teaching is largely irrelevant to growth in discipleship. Because of this view of faith and reason, there has emerged a secular-sacred separation in our understanding of the Christian life with the result that Christian teaching and practice are privatized. The withdrawal of the corporate body of Christ from the public sphere of ideas is mirrored by our understanding of what is required to produce an individual disciple. Religion is viewed as personal, private and a matter of how we feel about things. Often, Bible classes and paracurricular Christian activities are not taken as academically serious aspects of the Christian school, nor are they integrated into the content of "secular" areas of teaching.

There is no time like the present to recapture the integrative task. Given the abandonment of monotheism, the ground is weakened for believing in the unity of truth. This is one reason why our *uni*versities are turning in to *multi*versities.[8] The fragmentation of secular education at all levels and its inability to define its purpose or gather together a coherent curriculum are symptoms of what happens when monotheism, especially Christian monotheism, is set aside. At this critical hour the Christian educator has something increasingly rare and distinctive to offer, and integration is at the heart of who we are as Christian educators.

---

[8]See Julie Reuben, *The Making of the Modern University* (Chicago: University of Chicago Press, 1996).

5. *The nature of spiritual warfare necessitates integration.* Today, spiritual warfare is widely misunderstood. Briefly, spiritual warfare is a conflict among persons—disembodied malevolent persons (demons and the devil), human beings, angels and God himself. So far, so good. But what is often overlooked is that this conflict among persons in two camps crucially involves a clash of ideas. Why? The conflict is about control, and persons control others by getting them to accept certain beliefs and emotions as correct, good and proper. This is precisely how the devil primarily works to destroy human beings and thwart God's work in history, namely, by influencing the idea structures in culture. That is why Paul makes the war of ideas central to spiritual conflict:

> For though we live in the world, we do not wage war as the world does. The weapons we fight with are not the weapons of the world. On the contrary, they have divine power to demolish strongholds. We demolish arguments and every pretension that sets itself up against the knowledge of God, and we take captive every thought to make it obedient to Christ. (2 Cor 10:3-5 NIV)

Spiritual warfare is largely, though not entirely, a war of ideas, and we fight bad, false ideas with better ones. That means that truth, reason, argumentation and so forth, from both Scripture and general revelation, are central weapons in the fight. Since the centers of education are the centers for dealing with ideas, they become the main location for spiritual warfare. Solid, intelligent integration, then, is part of our mandate to engage in spiritual conflict.

6. *Spiritual formation calls for integration.* It is crucial that we reflect a bit on the relationship between integration and spiritual/devotional life. To begin with, there is a widespread hunger throughout our culture for genuine, life-transforming spirituality. This is as it should be. People are weary of those who claim to believe certain things when they do not see those beliefs having an impact on the lives of the heralds. Among other things, integration is a spiritual activity—we may even call it a spiritual discipline—but not merely in the sense that often comes to mind in this context. Often, Christian teachers express the spiritual aspect of integration in terms of doxology: Christian integra-

tors hold to and teach the same beliefs about their subject matter that non-Christians accept but go on to add praise to God for the subject matter. Thus, Christian biologists simply assert the views widely accepted in the discipline but make sure that class closes with a word of praise to God for the beauty and complexity of the living world.

The doxological approach is good as far as it goes; unfortunately, it doesn't go far enough in capturing the spiritual dimension of integration. We draw closer to the core of this dimension when we think about the role of beliefs in the process of spiritual transformation. Beliefs are the rails on which our lives run. We almost always act according to what we really believe. It doesn't matter much what we say we believe or what we want others to think we believe. When the rubber meets the road, we act out our actual beliefs most of the time. That is why behavior is such a good indicator of our beliefs. The centrality of beliefs for spiritual progress is a clear implication of Old Testament teaching on wisdom and New Testament teaching about the role of a renewed mind in transformation. Thus, *integration has as its spiritual aim the intellectual goal of structuring the mind so we can see things as they really are and strengthening the belief structure that ought to inform the individual and corporate life of discipleship to Jesus.*

Integration can also help unbelievers accept certain beliefs crucial to the Christian journey and aid believers in maintaining and developing convictions about those beliefs. This aspect of integration becomes clear when we reflect on the notion of a plausibility structure. Individuals will never be able to change their lives if they cannot even entertain the beliefs needed to bring about that change. By "entertain a belief" we mean to consider the *possibility* that the belief *might* be true. If someone is hateful and mean to a fellow employee, that person will have to change what he or she believes about that coworker before treating the coworker differently. But if a person cannot even entertain the thought that the coworker is a good person worthy of kindness, the hateful person will not change.

A person's plausibility structure is the set of ideas the person either is or is not willing to entertain as possibly true. For example, few people would come to a lecture defending a flat earth, because this idea is just not part of our common plausibility structure. Most people today simply cannot even entertain the idea. Moreover, a person's plausibility structure is largely (though not exclusively) a function of beliefs already held. Applied to accepting or maintaining Christian belief, J. Gresham Machen got it right when he said:

> God usually exerts that power in connection with certain prior conditions of the human mind, and it should be ours to create, so far as we can, with the help of God, those favorable conditions for the reception of the gospel. False ideas are the greatest obstacles to the reception of the gospel. We may preach with all the fervor of a reformer and yet succeed only in winning a straggler here and there, if we permit the whole collective thought of the nation or of the world to be controlled by ideas which, by the resistless force of logic, prevent Christianity from being regarded as anything more than a harmless delusion.[9]

If a culture reaches the point where Christian claims are not even part of its plausibility structure, fewer and fewer people will be able to entertain the possibility that they might be true. Whatever stragglers do come to faith in such a context would do so on the basis of felt needs alone, and the genuineness of such conversions would be questionable, to say the least. And believers will not make much progress in the spiritual life because they will not have the depth of conviction or the integrated noetic structure necessary for such progress. This is why integration is so crucial to spirituality. It can create a plausibility structure in a person's mind, "favorable conditions," as Machen put it, so Christian ideas can be entertained by that person. As Christians, our goal is *to make Christian ideas relevant to our subject matter appear to be true, beautiful, good and reasonable to increase the ranking of Christian ideas in the culture's plausibility structure.*

7. *Integration is crucial to the current worldview struggle and the contemporary crisis of knowledge.* Luther once said that if we defend Christ at all points except those at which he is currently being attacked, then we have not really defended Christ. The Christian must keep in mind the

---

[9]J. Gresham Machen, address delivered on September 20, 1912, at the opening of the 101st session of Princeton Theological Seminary, reprinted in *What Is Christianity?* (Grand Rapids: Eerdmans, 1951), p. 162.

tensions between Christian claims and competing worldviews currently dominating the culture. Such vigilance yields an integrative mandate for contemporary Christians that the Christian Worldview Integration Series (CWIS) will keep in mind. There is a very important cultural fact that each volume in the series must face: *There simply is no established, widely recognized body of ethical or religious knowledge now operative in the institutions of knowledge in our culture.* Indeed, ethical and religious claims are frequently placed into what Francis Schaeffer called the "upper story," and they are judged to have little or no epistemic authority, especially compared to the authority given to science to define the limits of knowledge and reality in those same institutions. This raises pressing questions: *Is Christianity a knowledge tradition or merely a faith tradition, a perspective which, while true, cannot be known to be true and must be embraced on the basis of some epistemic state weaker than knowledge? Is there nonempirical knowledge in my field? Is there evidence of nonphysical, immaterial reality (e.g., linguistic meanings are arguable, nonphysical, spiritual entities) in my field? Do the ideas of Christianity do any serious intellectual work in my field such that those who fail to take them into consideration simply will not be able to understand adequately the realities involved in my field?*

There are at least two reasons why these may well be the crucial questions for Christians to keep in mind as they do their work in their disciplines. For one thing, Christianity claims to be a knowledge tradition, and it places knowledge at the center of proclamation and discipleship. The Old and New Testaments, including the teachings of Jesus, claim not merely that Christianity is true but that a variety of its moral and religious assertions can be known to be true.

Second, knowledge is the basis of responsible action in society. Dentists, not lawyers, have the authority to place their hands in our mouths because they have the relevant knowledge—not merely true beliefs—on the basis of which they may act responsibly. If Christians do little to deflect the view that theological and ethical assertions are merely parts of a tradition, ways of seeing, a source for adding a "theological perspective" to an otherwise unperturbed secular topic and so forth that fall short of conveying knowledge, then they inadvertently contribute to the marginalization of Christianity precisely because they fail to rebut the contemporary tendency to rob it of the very thing that gives it the authority necessary to prevent that marginalization, namely, its legitimate claim to give us moral and religious knowledge. Both in and out of the church Jesus has been lost as an intellectual authority, and Christian intellectuals should carry out their academic vocation in light of this fact.

We agree with those who see a three-way worldview struggle in academic and popular culture among ethical monotheism (especially Christian theism), postmodernism and scientific naturalism. As Christian intellectuals seek to promote Christianity as a knowledge tradition in their academic disciplines, they should keep in mind the impact of their work on this triumvirate. Space considerations forbid us to say much about postmodernism here. We recognize it is a variegated tunic with many nuances. But to the degree that postmodernism denies the objectivity of reality, truth, value and reason (in its epistemic if not psychological sense), to the degree that it rejects dichotomous thinking about real-unreal, true-false, rational-irrational and right-wrong, to the degree that it believes intentionality creates the objects of consciousness, to that degree it should be resisted by Christian intellectuals, and the CWIS will take this stance toward postmodernism.

Scientific naturalism also comes in many varieties, but very roughly a major form of it is the view that the spatiotemporal cosmos containing physical objects studied by the hard sciences is all there is and that the hard sciences are either the only source of knowledge or else vastly superior in proffering epistemically justified beliefs compared to nonscientific fields. In connection with scientific naturalism some have argued that the rise of modern science has contributed to the loss of intellectual authority in those fields like ethics and religion that supposedly are not subject to the types of testing and experimentation employed in science.

Extreme forms of postmodernism and scientific naturalism agree that there is no nonempirical knowledge, especially no knowledge of immaterial reality, no theological or ethical knowledge. *The authors of the CWIS seek to undermine this claim and the concomitant privatization*

and noncognitive treatment of religious/ethical faith and belief. Thus, there
will be three integrative tasks of central importance for each volume in
the series.

HOW DO WE ENGAGE IN INTEGRATION? THREE INTEGRATIVE TASKS

As noted earlier, the word *integration* means "to form or blend into a
whole," "to unite." One of the goals of integration is to maintain or increase both the conceptual relevance of and epistemological justification for Christian theism. To repeat Augustine's advice, "We must
show our Scriptures not to be in conflict with whatever [our critics] can
demonstrate about the nature of things from reliable sources."[10] We
may distinguish three different aspects of the justificatory side of integration: direct defense, polemics and Christian explanation.

1. *Direct defense.* In direct defense we engage in integration with the
primary intent of enhancing or maintaining directly the rational justification of Christian theism or some proposition taken to be explicit
within or entailed by it, especially those aspects of a Christian worldview relevant to our own discipline. Specific attention should be given
to topics that are intrinsically important to mere Christianity or currently under fire in our field. Hereafter, we will simply refer to these
issues as "Christian theism." We do so for brevity's sake. Christian theism should be taken to include specific views about a particular area of
study that we believe to be relevant to the integrative task, for example,
that cognitive behavioral therapy is an important tool for applying the
biblical mandate to be "transformed by the renewing of your mind"
(Rom 12:2).

There are two basic forms of direct defense, one negative and one
positive.[11] The less controversial of the two is a negative direct defense
where we attempt to remove defeaters to Christian theism. If we have a
justified belief regarding some proposition P, a defeater is something
that weakens or removes that justification. Defeaters come in two
types.[12] A rebutting defeater gives justification for believing not-P, in

---

[10]Augustine *De genesi ad litteram* 1.21.
[11]See Ronald Nash, *Faith and Reason* (Grand Rapids: Zondervan, 1988), pp. 14-18.
[12]For a useful discussion of various types of defeaters, see John Pollock, *Contemporary Theories of*

this case, that Christian theism is false. For example, attempts to show that the biblical concept of the family is dysfunctional and false, or that homosexuality is causally necessitated by genes or brain states and that therefore it is not a proper object for moral appraisal are cases of rebutting defeaters. An undercutting defeater does not give justification for believing not-P but rather seeks to remove or weaken justification for believing P in the first place. Critiques of the arguments for God's existence are examples of undercutting defeaters. When defeaters are raised against Christian theism, a negative defense seeks either to rebut or undercut those defeaters.

By contrast, a positive direct defense is an attempt to build a positive case for Christian theism. Arguments for the existence of God, objective morality, the existence of the soul, the value and nature of virtue ethics, and the possibility and knowability of miracles are examples. This task for integration is not accepted by all Christian intellectuals. For example, various species of what may be loosely called Reformed epistemology run the gamut from seeing a modest role for a positive direct defense to an outright rejection of this type of activity in certain areas; for example, justifying belief in God and the authority of Holy Scripture. *The CWIS will seek to engage in both negative and positive direct defense.*

2. *Polemics.* In polemics we seek to criticize views that rival Christian theism in one way or another. Critiques of scientific naturalism, physicalism, pantheism, behaviorist models of educational goals, authorless approaches to texts and Marxist theories of economics are all examples of polemics.

3. *Theistic explanation.* Suppose we have a set of items that stand in need of explanation and we offer some overall explanation as an adequate or even best explanation of those items. In such a case our overall explanation explains each of the items in question, and this fact itself provides some degree of confirmation for our overall explanation. For example, if a certain intrinsic genre statement explains the various data of a biblical text, then this fact offers some confirmation

---

Knowledge (Totowa, N.J.: Rowman & Littlefield, 1986), pp. 36-39; Ralph Baergen, *Contemporary Epistemology* (Fort Worth: Harcourt Brace, 1995), pp. 119-24.

for the belief that the statement is the correct interpretation of that text. Christian theists ought to be about the business of exploring the world in light of their worldview and, more specifically, of using their theistic beliefs as explanations of various desiderata in their disciplines. Put differently, we should seek to solve intellectual problems and shed light on areas of puzzlement by using the explanatory power of our worldview.

For example, for those who accept the existence of natural moral law, the irreducibly mental nature of consciousness, natural human rights or the fact that human flourishing follows from certain biblically mandated ethical and religious practices, the truth of Christian theism provides a good explanation of these phenomena. And this fact can provide some degree of confirmation for Christian theism. *The CWIS seeks to show the explanatory power of Christian ideas in various disciplines.*

WHAT MODELS ARE AVAILABLE FOR CLASSIFYING INTEGRATIVE PROBLEMS?

When problem areas surface, there is a need for Christians to think hard about the issue in light of the need for strengthening the rational authority of Christian theism and placing it squarely within the plausibility structure of contemporary culture. We will use the term *theology* to stand for any Christian idea that seems to be a part of a Christian worldview derived primarily from special revelation. When we address problems like these, there will emerge a number of different ways that theology can interact with an issue in a discipline outside theology. Here are some of the different ways that such interaction can take place. These represent different strategies for handling a particular difficulty in integration. These strategies will be employed where appropriate on a case-by-case basis by the authors in the series.

1. *The two-realms view.* Propositions, theories or methodologies in theology and another discipline may involve two distinct, nonoverlapping areas of investigation. For example, debates about angels or the extent of the atonement have little to do with organic chemistry. Similarly, it is of little interest to theology whether a methane molecule has three or four hydrogen atoms in it.

2. *The complementarity view.* Propositions, theories or methodologies in theology and another discipline may involve two different, complementary, noninteracting approaches to the same reality. Sociological aspects of church growth and certain psychological aspects of conversion may be sociological or psychological descriptions of certain phenomena that are complementary to a theological description of church growth or conversion.

3. *The direct-interaction view.* Propositions, theories or methodologies in theology and another discipline may directly interact in such a way that either one area of study offers rational support for the other or one area of study raises rational difficulties for the other. For example, certain theological teachings about the existence of the soul raise rational problems for philosophical or scientific claims that deny the existence of the soul. The general theory of evolution raises various difficulties for certain ways of understanding the book of Genesis. Some have argued that the big bang theory tends to support the theological proposition that the universe had a beginning.

4. *The presuppositions view.* Theology may support the presuppositions of another discipline and vice versa. Some have argued that many of the presuppositions of science (for example, the existence of truth; the rational, orderly nature of reality; the adequacy of our sensory and cognitive faculties as tools suited for knowing the external world) make sense and are easy to justify given Christian theism, but are odd and without ultimate justification in a naturalistic worldview. Similarly, some have argued that philosophical critiques of epistemological skepticism and defenses of the existence of a real, theory-independent world and a correspondence theory of truth offer justification for some of the presuppositions of theology.

5. *The practical application view.* Theology may fill out and add details to general principles in another discipline and vice versa, and theology may help us practically apply principles in another discipline and vice versa. For example, theology teaches that fathers should not provoke their children to anger, and psychology can add important details about what this means by offering information about family systems, the nature and causes of anger, and so forth. Psychology can devise

various tests for assessing whether a person is or is not mature, and theology can offer a normative definition to psychology as to what a mature person is.

Since the early 1980s conservative Christians have become far more active in American politics than they were in prior decades. This has been largely attributed to the ascendancy of secular understandings of the public square that many Christians believe seek to exclude religious voices. In this book, *Politics for Christians,* the author discusses how Christians should think about their role in the public square. He argues that liberal democracy, properly understood, permits Christians to influence and shape their nation's political and cultural institutions in order to advance the common good. Moreover, the liberties we cherish—such as the freedoms of speech, religion and association—seem to depend on a natural moral law that is best explained by the existence of God. The author introduces the reader to the study of politics by exploring several issues central to a Christian engagement in politics: the discipline of politics, liberal democracy and the Christian citizen, separation of church and state, secular liberalism and the neutral state, and God and natural rights.

We hope you can see why we are excited about this book. Even though you're busy and the many demands on your time tug at you from different directions, we don't think you can afford not to read this book. So wrestle, ponder, pray, compare ideas with Scripture, talk about the pages to follow with others and enjoy.

A FINAL CHALLENGE

In 2001 atheist philosopher Quentin Smith published a remarkably insightful article of crucial relevance to the task of integration. For over fifty years, Smith notes, the academic community has become increasingly secularized and atheistic even though there have been a fair number of Christian teachers involved in that community. How could this be? Smith's answer amounts to the claim that Christians compartmentalized their faith, kept it tucked away in a private compartment of their lives and did not integrate their Christian ideas with their work. Said Smith:

This is not to say that none of the scholars in their various academic fields were realist theists [theists who took their religious beliefs to be true] in their "private lives"; but realist theists, for the most part excluded their theism from their publications and teaching, in large part because theism . . . was mainly considered to have such a low epistemic status that it did not meet the standards of an "academically respectable" position to hold.[13]

Smith goes on to claim that while Christians have recaptured considerable ground in the field of philosophy, "theists in other fields tend to compartmentalize their theistic beliefs from their scholarly work; they rarely assume and never argue for theism in their scholarly work."[14]

This has got to stop. We offer this book to you with the prayer that it will help you rise to the occasion and recapture lost territory in your field of study for the cause of Christ.

Francis J. Beckwith
J. P. Moreland
Series Editors

---

[13]Quentin Smith, "The Metaphysics of Naturalism," *Philo* 4, no. 2 (2001): 1.
[14]Ibid., p. 3. The same observation about advances in philosophy has been noted by Mark A. Noll in *The Scandal of the Evangelical Mind* (Grand Rapids: Eerdmans, 1994), pp. 235-38.

ACKNOWLEDGMENTS

My understanding of politics is the result of influences from many quarters in the academy including philosophy, political science, theology and law. Without these predecessors and contemporaries, my thoughts would have remained undeveloped and my scholarship incomplete. Although I could mention many others, I would like to single out the following scholars who have made the most significant contributions to my intellectual development: Hadley Arkes, William F. Buckley Jr., Robert P. George, Francis Canavan, S. J., Christopher Wolfe, Michael Sandel, Arthur Leff, John Warwick Montgomery, George Gilder, Stephen Monsma, Murray Rothbard, George Will, Louis P. Pojman, Michael Bauman, Stephen Carter, Phillip E. Johnson, Michael Novak, Phillip Hamburger, Robert Cord, Michael McConnell, James V. Schall, S. J., Luis Lugo, Douglas Kimec and J. Budziszewski. Thank you.

Before I moved to Baylor University's philosophy department in June 2007, from 2003 through 2007 I was an associate professor in Baylor's department of church-state studies and associate director of its J. M. Dawson Institute of Church-State Studies. During those four years I had the privilege of working with many fine students in the department's doctoral programs. Four of these students—T. Hunter Baker, John Lee, Jeremiah Russell and Gerard Figurelli—served as my graduate assistants and worked closely with me on several projects that helped to form the ideas in this book. I would like to thank them for their wonderful questions and insights. My current department chair, Michael Beaty, has been especially supportive of my work and was instrumental in helping to secure for me a Baylor research leave for the 2008-2009 school year so that I could complete this book as well as work on another project. During that year, I served on the faculty of the University of Notre Dame as the Mary Ann Remick Senior Visiting Fellow in the Center for Ethics and Culture. I would like to thank the center's director, W. David Solomon, as well as its associate directors, Elizabeth Kirk and Daniel McInerny (who is now a professor in Baylor's Honors College), for providing me with the opportunity to have a productive year in an idyllic environment with outstanding colleagues that included Alasdair McIntyre and Sarah Borden (a philosopher from Wheaton College who was the other visiting fellow for 2008-2009).

Finally, no one deserves more recognition and more praise than my beautiful wife, Frankie. She not only manages my schedule, books my speaking engagements and keeps our financial affairs in order, but she also reminds me, by example and instruction, that the most important things have their patrimony in that which is eternal and unchanging. Without her, my life would surely be impoverished.

Earlier versions of parts of this book were published elsewhere as portions of the following articles, but have been revised, and in some cases significantly revised, for inclusion in this present volume:

"Bioethics, the Christian Citizen, and the Pluralist Game," *Christian Bioethics* 13 (2007): 159-70.

"Is it Permissible for a Christian to Vote for a Mormon?" *Christian Research Journal* 30, no. 5 (2007) <www.equip.org/PDF/JAM511.pdf>.

"The Courts, Natural Rights and Religious Claims as Knowledge," *Santa Clara Law Review* 49, no. 2 (Fall 2008): 429-58.

"Gimme That Ol' Time Separation: A Review Essay of Separation of Church and State by Philip Hamburger," *Chapman Law Review* 8, no. 1 (2005): 109-27. A later, revised version, also appeared as "Christians, Politics, and the Separation of Church and State," in *Reasons for Faith*, ed. Norman L. Geisler and Chad Meister (Wheaton, Ill.: Crossway Books, 2007), pp. 127-41.

"Are There Limits to Religious Free Exercise?" *Christian Research Journal* 28, no. 5 (2005): 52-53.

I would like to thank the publishers and editors of the above publications not only for allowing my work to appear in print in these venues, but also for permitting me to republish revised portions of those works here.

INTRODUCTION

Politics" is derived from the Greek word for city, *polis*. The study of politics is, therefore, an attempt to understand "the city," the inner workings of a community and the way by which it governs itself over time. The governed are called "citizens," and those who do the governing are part of the government, the entity that makes, enforces and applies the laws. So students of politics must concern themselves with knowing what it means to be a citizen as well as whether the government under which these citizens live is just or unjust. Because the Christian tradition—both in its Scripture and in the writings of its great teachers—has addressed questions pertaining to citizenship and the administration of justice, Christian students of politics have a reservoir of wisdom at their disposal.

The primary purpose of this book is to introduce the Christian student to the study of politics. I pay particular attention to addressing the legitimate concern of many citizens that religious citizens, including Christian ones, should set aside their beliefs before they enter the public square. I also hope to provide the Christian student with an account of politics and government that includes an understanding and appreciation of liberal democracy that is not hostile to Christian participation and the shaping of public policy.

Too often the study of politics from a Christian perspective comes across as politics plus the Bible, as if Scripture is the entirety of Christian thinking and that it is a mere afterthought that contributes nothing to our knowledge of politics. What I mean by this is that oftentimes Christians treat the Bible as a collection of proof-texts that

simply serve to confirm in their minds what they already believe on
other grounds. So, for example, conservative Christians "find" free
markets in Scripture, while liberal Christians "find" the welfare state.
And rarely do such Christians entertain the possibility that their
reading of Scripture is colored by certain assumptions about the human person, property and freedom that are completely alien to the
biblical worldview. I offer this book, though only an introduction, as
a correction to this approach to Christianity and politics. That is, if
Christians believe that Christianity is true in all that it affirms about
human beings, justice, the good life, and the kindness and love owed
to non-Christian neighbors, then any politics that does not take into
consideration these truths will never be complete. Of course, in a
sense, given fallen human nature, no political system or government
is ever really complete this side of eternity. For this reason, Christians
must strive to be humble and teachable and to nurture in their souls
the Christian virtues as they offer their claims to a world that, in
some of its locales, has grown increasingly unreceptive to Christianity and what it affirms.

Moreover, Christians who uncritically look to Scripture for guidance
in politics run the risk of treating the church at one point in its history
(usually the first century) as the norm for the church's political involvement for all of history. Although, as I argue in chapter two, the Bible
does indeed offer principles for human conduct that may be applied
universally and across time to a variety of political regimes, one must
exercise care in extracting those principles from a church that was in its
infancy and whose members were without any real political or cultural
influence. Compare that church with the fourth-century church, which
had become a dominant force in the Roman Empire. Christianity was
attracting converts from every walk of life and profession. Thus, unlike
their first-century counterparts, the fourth-century church and its
members actually had to wrestle with issues having to do with the
proper exercise of political, social and cultural power. They really had
no choice. They could not just let the pagans run things, since the pagan world and its influence were rapidly diminishing. Christians themselves had to figure out how to run things. Although they, like Chris-

tians today, had the resource of Scripture, they did not have the benefit of two millennia of Christian reflection on church and state. This is not to say that the church has not made political mistakes throughout its history. It most certainly has. Rather, what I am suggesting is that each generation of Christians has to rethink the church's role in the political realm, with reliance on Scripture coupled with an appropriate, though not slavish, deference to the insights of our predecessors. This is because each generation faces new and different challenges that its ancestors could not have anticipated. Nevertheless, each subsequent generation has a larger reservoir of resources (including the church's successes as well as its tragic political mistakes) at its disposal in comparison to its immediate antecedent.

A PERSONAL PILGRIMAGE

My parents, Harold ("Pat") and Elizabeth Beckwith, exposed me to the importance of politics and citizenship at an early age. And for that, I am so thankful. In the mid-1960s, they had my brother James and me watch important political events and speeches. In 1968, when I was seven years old, I distinctly remember watching and listening to Robert F. Kennedy on the evening he was assassinated in Los Angeles, and seeing my parents cry when his death was announced on our television hours later. Only months earlier, Martin Luther King Jr. had been murdered in Memphis. My parents supported the civil rights movement and were diligent in making sure that my brother and I knew of Dr. King and the tragedy of his death. Although I was too young to remember the presidency of John F. Kennedy, my father made sure we listened to the late president's 1961 inaugural address, one of the great political speeches in American history. On several occasions, my father played the recording of Kennedy's speech on our old family turntable. Thus, it is not a coincidence that in a class I teach, American Civil Religion, I have had my Baylor graduate students read Kennedy's address along with the important speeches of Presidents Abraham Lincoln, Franklin Delano Roosevelt, Ronald W. Reagan and George W. Bush. My father also had a sense of humor about politics. When I was eight years old I asked him to explain to me the difference between communism and capitalism. He answered, "Well, son, in America, a capitalist country, some people own Cadillacs and some people don't. But in communist countries like the Soviet Union, everyone is treated equally; no one owns a Cadillac."

For a time during my middle school years, I returned home every afternoon to see my mother watching the Watergate Hearings, chaired by one of her heroes, Senator Sam Ervin (D-SC). She always invited me to join her, which I did almost always. I was fascinated by the hearings, the issues surrounding them and the historical importance of all the figures who were participating. As I grew older and began to develop my own political opinions, my parents exhibited an exemplary level of tolerance and openness. To be sure, we had times of vigorous debate, but we had passionate agreements as well. Always, we learned from each other in a context of respect and understanding.

Consequently, because my own intellectual and spiritual formation was accompanied by an interest in politics, the notion that statecraft is soulcraft seems to me irresistibly true. I understand that others have not had this good fortune. For this reason, this introductory text makes the case that statecraft *is* soulcraft.

STATECRAFT AS SOULCRAFT

"Statecraft," Aristotle instructed his pupils, "is soulcraft." He meant by this that the state or government, by its policies, procedures and actions, places moral ideas in the social and legal fabric of a political regime, and that these ideas serve to shape the quality of its citizens' character. This central truth animates the notion of politics offered in this book. And it is, I will argue, central to a Christian understanding of politics.

Those who live in a liberal democracy, such as the United States of America or the United Kingdom, are blessed with the power to shape their communities through the ordinances of government. Liberal democracy provides citizens with the opportunity to pass laws and support policies that they believe are just, fair and advance the common good. For example, some Christians believe that most abortions ought to be illegal because the unborn are persons and thus ought to be protected under law from unjustified homicide in the same way the laws protect postnatal citizens and noncitizens. Some Christians also believe that because the natural world is a gift from God, human beings are in a unique position to nurture and protect it. Thus, they argue, the government ought to pass laws that forbid the pollution of the environment and that protect species whose endangerment is the result of human excess and greed. But these sorts of policies, though they appear good to many Christians (and some non-Christians as well), are resisted by other citizens who believe that such apparently religiously based beliefs should not be the basis of any laws in a secular society such as the United States, whose Constitution forbids the establishment of religion in government.

Many, though not all, Christians see this call for excluding their public voices as inconsistent with another important principle of liberal democracy, namely, that citizens ought to be treated equally under the law, which means that their political participation should not depend on their willingness to set aside their religious beliefs. To be more precise, many Christians think they have good reason to believe that in the conflicts over controversial political issues, such as abortion, same-sex marriage, physician-assisted suicide and embryonic stem-cell research, there does not seem to be a level playing field. Perspectives that appear antithetical to the Christian tradition seem to be treated by some as default positions, requiring no argument or case.

It is true, of course, that Christians hold a variety of points of view on the issues I have mentioned. For this reason, someone may raise the legitimate question as to why I am stressing those positions that are embraced by Christians who are politically conservative. Here's why: many Christians who embrace liberal positions on issues such as same-sex marriage, abortion, physician-assisted suicide and embryonic stem-cell research claim that their religious traditions provide them with a framework that requires them to hold these views, but they are rarely, if ever, challenged for mixing religion with politics. And when the views of some otherwise conservative Christians overlap those of many liberal Christians and non-Christians (e.g., environmentalism, no public funding for faith-based initiatives, prohibiting teacher-led prayer in public schools), those conservative Christians are not challenged as they are when they defend the prolife view on abortion, traditional marriage or the protection of embryos as research subjects.

THE SCOPE OF THIS BOOK

I first introduce the student to the study of politics (chapter 1). In this chapter I cover a number of areas of study that colleges and universities place in what are called *departments of political science, politics* or *government*. In chapter two I define and explain the meaning of the term *liberal democracy* and then address the question of how Christians should look at the study of politics and what insights they can bring to their communities.

In the next three chapters I address three issues over which Christians and non-Christians have wrestled (or ought to wrestle) and which are important questions in the study of politics. In chapter three I address the issue of the separation of church and state. Although those precise words are not found in the U.S. Constitution, as even defenders of church-state separation readily admit, some people argue that the principles of the Constitution in fact support the notion that church and state ought to be separate. That seems to me to be uncontroversial, and virtually no one defends uniting church and state. After all, the Constitution both asserts a right to religious free exercise and prohibits the government from establishing a religion. But why then is there such debate about this? It is because no one can agree on precisely what the separation of church and state means. Also in chapter three I defend a legal view that supports religious liberty, while at the same time allows religious citizens the opportunity to make a public case for their views, that does not give an unjust preference to secular points of view claimed by proponents to be "neutral."

The focus of chapter four is the relationship of the ideals of liberal democracy to the political participation of the Christian citizen. For example, because many Christians (and many non-Christians as well) believe that communities, just like rainforests and natural habitats, have an ecology that can be harmed (what is sometimes called a "moral ecology"[1]), they have attempted to pass, and in some cases have passed,

---

[1]Robert P. George, *Making Men Moral: Civil Liberties and Public Morality* (New York: Oxford University Press, 1993), p. 37.

laws that either forbid, limit, restrict, regulate or condemn certain conduct (e.g., the distribution of obscene materials). Is it right for citizens in a liberal democracy to do this, or do such laws infringe on the liberty of other citizens who reject the morality on which these laws are based? On issues such as the funding of embryonic stem-cell research, same-sex marriage, abortion, physician-assisted suicide and human cloning, one often hears the claim that attempts to restrict such conduct, especially if the restriction is borne of a religious worldview, is an inappropriate attempt on the part of some citizens to force their morality on others and, thus, is inconsistent with the idea of liberal democracy. This is because those who hold this view believe that the liberal democratic state should remain neutral on matters over which reasonable citizens disagree. In chapter four I argue that this view is mistaken because the state cannot in fact remain neutral on matters of worldview.

I address in chapter five the question of whether liberal democracy requires a theistic worldview in order to account for the intrinsic dignity and natural rights of human beings that liberal democracy seems to require. It is well known that America's Declaration of Independence asserts that our rights are inalienable and "self-evident" and "endowed" to us by our "Creator."[2] But is God really necessary for grounding natural rights and the natural moral law that supports them? Some philosophers and political and legal theorists argue that Darwinian evolution can account just as well for natural moral law and natural rights, and thus there is no need to require God's existence. I critique this view and conclude that the existence of natural rights is based on a natural moral law that is best accounted for by the existence of a God who is the source of the natural moral law.

This book is not meant to be a scholarly monograph that defends as correct a particular understanding of liberal democracy and its relationship to Christianity. Rather, my purpose is to introduce the college student to politics by way of a few issues and questions that should be of concern to contemporary Christian citizens in liberal democracies. To be sure, I suggest ways of understanding these issues and questions

---

[2]U.S. Declaration of Independence (1776), par. 2.

that I believe are consistent both with liberal democracy and the truth of the Christian message. I know that a few of my colleagues will disagree with some, if not all, of my suggestions. Having said that, I believe that this text is a reasonable way to introduce students to the study of politics and serves as a modest word in the continued conversation among Christian and non-Christian scholars on the proper role of religious citizens and their beliefs in a liberal democracy.

In order to be wise stewards of the gift of self-government in a liberal democracy, Christians must understand not only what their theology teaches about their obligations to the wider community of human persons but also to understand both the nature of their government and its politics. Christians have to be, in the words of Jesus, "wise as serpents, and harmless as doves" (Mt 10:16 ASV). It is my hope that this book will contribute to your understanding of politics and Christianity.

THE STUDY OF POLITICS

Imagine that you are sitting in church on Sunday morning. Your minister preaches an out-of-the-ordinary sermon. Instead of his usual discussions of Scripture, theology or Christian spirituality, he instructs the members of his congregation to petition their local county commissioners to vote against an ordinance that would force all businesses in the community to offer benefits to same-sex couples if the business offers benefits to married heterosexual couples. He explains to you and your fellow churchgoers that the Bible condemns homosexuality and, therefore, Christians have a duty to make sure that the government does not promote this lifestyle. Even though you agree with your minister's rendering of Scripture, you are not quite sure that it would be right for you to try to influence public policy based on the Bible. After all, you reason (if you are an American), the U.S. Constitution requires a separation of church and state, and would not a scriptural justification of a public policy violate what the Constitution requires? On the other hand, you are a business owner who has several homosexual employees whose competence in their jobs you have no doubt, and for that reason, you have no intention to terminate their employment because of their homosexuality. However, you do not want to provide benefits for a lifestyle that you believe is deeply immoral. It is one thing for the state to prohibit a uniting of church and state, but why should you, a faithful Christian, have to acquiesce to the state's demands that your business support something that your faith maintains is immoral? If mixing church and state is bad, as you have been told numerous times by close friends, why don't these same friends see a bad mix when the state instructs the church and its members on how to conduct their businesses when the matters at hand have historically been the domain of the church and its theology?

Whether we like it or not, Christians in a liberal democracy will face these and many other political questions throughout their adult lives. The issues involve questions about which candidate to vote for, what political party to join, what causes to support, how much a minister should speak of politics in the pulpit, how one should deal with fellow Christians who are political adversaries, and to what extent one should become involved in local politics (including, for example, school boards, city councils and ballot measures). But in order to address these questions, one must have a framework in which to assess them, just as one cannot understand a basketball game without knowing the rules and the different roles that the participants play (e.g., coach, referee, player), their assigned positions (e.g., center, forward, trainer), and the varied tasks they perform. To answer questions Christians may have about politics, such as those suggested above, we need to understand first what politics is and why it is permissible for a Christian to be active in studying and shaping political discourse.

However, as should be obvious, that is not all we need to know. After all, the questions with which Christians most frequently deal—in the church, the public square and the academic world—concern issues such as the proper relationship between church and state, whether the form of government (usually, liberal democracy) is consistent with (or perhaps, more strongly, justified by) Christian beliefs, or whether it is ever permissible to legislate "Christian" morality in a pluralistic society. These and other questions will be assessed in chapters two through five. But we have to start somewhere. And the best place to start is at the beginning. Thus, we will first—in this present chapter—explore the academic discipline of politics. We will then in the next chapter provide reasons why a Christian may study politics and/or become an active participant in it.

POLITICS AND ITS SUBFIELDS

Nearly every university and college includes a department or school that deals exclusively with the study of politics. They are usually designated as *departments* or *schools of political science*, though at many institutions they go by different names such as *politics* or *government*. But those are not the only places at the university in which one may study politics. Departments and schools of philosophy, history, public policy, public affairs, sociology and law deal with politics in one way or another, often offering courses that address specific areas or issues of politics and government. One is also likely to come across courses that specifically address political issues, or contain readings and lessons that delve into matters of politics, in departments and schools of theology, English, religion, medicine, communication studies and psychology. The study of politics runs through the academy; one need not be a political science or government major in order to have a serious academic interest in politics. My own academic training is in philosophy (Ph.D., Fordham) and law (M.J.S., Washington University School of Law, St. Louis), and I have been a faculty member in departments, schools or centers of politics (Princeton), law (Trinity Law School), philosophy (University of Nevada-Las Vegas, Whittier, Baylor), theology (Trinity Evangelical Divinity School), church-state studies (Baylor), and ethics and culture (University of Notre Dame).

Like other disciplines in the academy, politics is an area of study that includes several subfields that sometimes overlap each other, as well as intersecting a variety of academic disciplines such as philosophy, history or law. So, for example, it is not unusual for a political science department to offer courses in political philosophy, jurisprudence, history of politics, political theology, political rhetoric or international human rights that are crosslisted with departments or schools of philosophy, law, history, theology, communication studies or international relations.

For its 2009 annual meeting, the American Political Science Association (APSA) listed forty-nine different divisions that correspond to subfields of study within that academic society.[1] In a survey of the distribution of specialties among its membership, the APSA lists eight subfields: public policy, public law and courts, political philosophy and theory, public administration, methodology, international politics,

---

[1]APSA Division Calls and Division Chair Contact Information page, American Political Science Association (2009) <www.apsanet.org/section_623.cfm>.

comparative politics, and American government and politics.[2] Thus, given these two lists from the leading academic society of political scientists, and given the modest goals of this book, we can not possibly review every subfield with the rigor and depth each undoubtedly deserves. Consequently, what follows is a brief overview of a few of the subfields within the study of politics that I believe may be of special interest to Christians. For this reason, this overview will appear unconventional to some, though not all, of my colleagues in political science departments. Nevertheless, because we are introducing Christian students to the study of politics, and because Christianity brings to bear on this study issues and questions that may be prioritized differently by those outside the church, the following brief overview of some subfields in politics should be understood with that in mind.

POLITICAL THEORY (OR POLITICAL PHILOSOPHY)

Political theory encompasses a multitude of philosophical questions about the nature of government, the individual, rights, democracy, liberty, equality and the good. For example, many political theorists have addressed this question: Is there such a thing as natural rights? The great English philosopher John Locke (1632-1704) answered yes to this question and then defended a form of government that he thought best protected these natural rights. These rights include the right to life, personal liberty and ownership of private property. According to Locke, God endows us with these rights, and a just government has an obligation to ensure that these rights are not trampled on by other citizens or by the government itself. The type of government suggested by Locke is often called "the separation of powers": a Constitutional democracy consisting of three branches—executive, legislative and judicial—that are coequal and check and balance each other. Because unaccountable human beings with too much power cannot be trusted to protect the rights of others, Locke thought that this form of government stood the best chance of resisting despotism and rampant injustice. If you have not noticed already,

---

[2]"Chart I. A. 3: Distribution of Major Fields, Current APSA Members," American Political Science Association (2008) <www.apsanet.org/imgtest/IA3.pdf>.

Locke's view strongly influenced the founders of the United States of America. (We will briefly discuss the notion of "separation of powers" in chapter 2.)

Assuming that Locke is correct about natural rights, are there instances of human choice and action that are not "rightful"? We can easily think of acts that people clearly do not have the right to perform, such as engaging in fraud, murder or burglary. But those are uncontroversial cases. What about cases in which there does not seem to be a victim, cases in which all the participants consent? Are there such cases that are still not rightful and may be legitimately prohibited by the government? Most citizens, jurists and politicians throughout history have thought so. Among them was Locke, who argues that liberty does not entail the right to destroy oneself or to sell oneself into slavery. Concerning the latter, he writes:

> This freedom from absolute, arbitrary power, is so necessary to, and closely joined with a man's preservation, that he cannot part with it, but by what forfeits his preservation and life together: for a man, not having the power of his own life, cannot, by compact, or his own consent, enslave himself to any one, nor put himself under the absolute, arbitrary power of another, to take away his life, when he pleases. No body can give more power than he has himself; and he that cannot take away his own life, cannot give another power over it.[3]

Consider a real-life example. In the United States, polygamy is forbidden in all fifty states. In fact, when Utah was still a territory, the federal government passed legislation that prohibited the practice of polygamy in all U.S. territories including Utah,[4] the territory that had been settled by thousands of Mormons who practiced polygamy. Soon after the law was passed, several Mormons were arrested under the statute. The case eventually made it to the U.S. Supreme Court, in which the attorneys for the Mormons argued that their clients had a First Amendment religious-free-exercise right to practice polygamy.

---

[3]John Locke, *Second Treatise on Government* (1690), chap. 3, sec. 23. Concerning the right to destroy oneself see ibid., chap. 2, sec. 6.

[4]*The Morrill Act of 1862*, 37th Cong., 2nd sess. (July 2, 1862), 12 Stat. 501; and *The Edmunds Act of 1882*, 47th Cong., 1st session (March 23, 1882) 22 Stat. 30.

After all, according to the First Amendment, "Congress shall make no law respecting an establishment of religion, or prohibiting the free exercise thereof." And was it not Congress that passed the law prohibiting the free exercise of the religiously commanded practice of polygamy?

In *Reynolds v. United States* (1878), the Supreme Court rejected the Mormons' free exercise argument on the grounds that even though "Congress was deprived of all legislative power over mere opinion, . . . [it] was left free to reach actions [such as polygamy] which were in violation of social duties or subversive of good order."[5] What the Court meant by this is that certain institutions and ways of life, such as marriage and the family, are essential to the preservation of civil society. The government may craft its laws in such a way that certain practices receive a privileged position in our social fabric, and actions contrary to them should be prohibited or at least discouraged even if they have religious sanction. In order to better understand what the Court was thinking, consider this example. Imagine if each bank in the United States could print its own currency. Although each bank would be, in a sense, freer than it was when it was mandated to use only the government's currency, in another sense, there would be less freedom. For the predictability, stability, confidence and efficiency that one currency brings to commerce would vanish. So, in this case, the freedom of individual banks would result in diminishing the common good and far less aggregate freedom. This is because an essential component for maintaining the good of society's infrastructure has been weakened. If you think of certain institutions (like marriage and the family) as essential components for maintaining society's common good, as no doubt the Reynolds Court thought, you can at least understand why the Court took the position that it did, even if you don't find yourself entirely persuaded by its reasoning.

So, according to the Court's understanding, which agrees with Locke's view of rights, the government may pass laws that limit wrong actions, laws that violate no one's rights, since no one has a right to do

---

[5]*Reynolds v. United States*, 98 U.S. 145 (1878), pp. 145, 164.

wrong. Of course, this understanding becomes more controversial when citizens disagree over whether or not the prohibited activity is itself a wrong and/or inconsistent with the public good. So, one may agree with Locke that no one has a right to do a wrong but disagree with those who say, for example, that homosexuality, abortion or pornography is a wrong. Or, one may very well think that these are wrongs but for other reasons believe that the government should not criminalize such activities.

These are not the only questions with which political theorists deal. Among the other areas into which political theorists delve are the purpose of government (Should government advance the human good or—because there is too much disagreement among reasonable people over what the human good is—make sure that the individual's desires are not hindered?), the meaning of justice (Is economic justice equality of opportunity or a distribution of resources according to a just pattern?), the nature of political equality (What does it mean to say that all citizens are equal under the law?), and the case for and against military action (Is this war just?).

Students in an introductory politics course are usually exposed to another area of interest for political theorists: different forms of government and how they are justified. Although most people reading this book are citizens of liberal democracies with a government of separated powers (such as the United States of America), there are liberal democracies with entwined and partially separated powers (such as the United Kingdom) and nations that are monarchies that do not (e.g., Saudi Arabia) and do (e.g., Monaco) enforce the principles of liberal democracy. There are also nations like Cuba and the former Nazi Germany that are and were dictatorships in which the legislative body of the government is under the thumb of the dictator and the rule of law is really the rule of the leader. Others are or have been under military rule (e.g., Franco's Spain, ancient Sparta).

Because the issues that interest political theorists touch on many questions about which Christian citizens are concerned, much of the material covered in this book may properly be placed under the heading of political theory.

COMPARATIVE POLITICS

As one would probably guess, comparative politics concerns the study of the world's differing political systems, forms of government and institutions by comparing them in order to answer a variety of questions about the societies and cultures in which these systems, governments and institutions exist. So, for example, a scholar of comparative politics may want to know about the possible social consequences of legalizing same-sex marriage in the United States by studying what has occurred in Denmark,[6] the first nation to legalize the practice in 1992. There are, of course, differences between the Danish and American cultures that may lead one to doubt whether the consequences of the Danish experiment can be legitimately employed in making predictions about what might happen in the United States. On the other hand, it depends on the differences. Because Denmark is much more homogenous than the United States, and because homogeneity lends itself to social stability, perhaps one can conclude that if Denmark's experiment has had undesirable consequences for Danish society, then the consequences of same-sex marriage for the United States may be worse given the absence of the stabilizing variable of homogeneity.

Although this sort of study will involve what is called quantitative research—vital statistics on marriage and divorce rates, abortion, child-rearing, out-of-wedlock births, etc.—it will also require what is called qualitative judgments. For example, suppose that a few years after Denmark legalized same-sex marriage, heterosexual marriage rates began to decline every year while divorce rates, abortions, single-parent homes and out-of-wedlock births moved annually in the opposite direction at an exponential rate. Suppose that a scholar were to conclude from this that America ought not legalize same-sex marriage in order to reduce the likelihood of the Danish consequences occurring in the United States. This policy suggestion assumes a judgment that is not in the statistics gathered: the Danish consequences are bad and thus undesir-

---

[6]This is precisely what Stanley Kurtz has done in his article, "The End of Marriage in Scandinavia: The 'Conservative Case' for Same-Sex Marriage Collapses," *The Weekly Standard* 9, no. 20 (Feb. 2, 2004): <www.weeklystandard.com/content/public/articles/000/000/003/660zypwj .asp?pg=1>.

able. In addition, the fact that the comparativist (as she or he is sometimes called) chooses to study this subject—marriage and family—rather than another subject assumes a qualitative judgment about the relative importance of certain institutions and practices in comparison to others. So, the comparativist must inevitably rely on nonquantitative judgments that are associated with political theory. That is, questions of good and bad, just and unjust, fair and unfair, and even metaphysical questions about human nature, liberty and the good life will play a role in the work of comparativists whether or not they realize it.

Comparativists interested in studying Denmark and the United States on the issue of same-sex marriage may also want to discover the beliefs of each nation's citizens on homosexuality and the nature of marriage. This will probably involve the use of surveys and polls in order to accumulate data so that the comparativist can offer a hypothesis, a theory that explains why there are contrary attitudes between the two countries. She may hypothesize that each nation's view on homosexuality is the result of citizens' beliefs about human nature, which in turn are shaped by their religious and philosophical beliefs. And thus, a comparative politics study could argue that it is more likely that Americans, far more influenced by their religious traditions than are Western Europeans, see homosexuality as immoral, since it is contrary to Scripture and/or natural law.

Scholars of comparative politics have a broad range of interests. One can find comparativists concentrating on geographical regions (e.g., Latin America), forms of government (e.g., Western democracies), political parties (e.g., social democrats in Germany and France), gender (e.g., the political status of women in Israel and Saudi Arabia), political philosophies (e.g., communism in China and the former Soviet Union), nongovernment institutions (e.g., the Catholic Church and the governments of Spain and Italy), social practices (e.g., marriage and family policies in the United States and the United Kingdom), and political economies (e.g., free markets in Taiwan and mainland China). The list can go on and on.

Comparative politics can be found in the Bible. The Old Testament records the history of Israel and its relation to and interaction with other societies, often comparing the Jewish people to its Middle Eastern neighbors. One also finds the prophets suggesting that political systems can be compared to one another in terms of how closely they practice principles of divine justice. Although it is difficult to find in the New Testament such specific cases of comparative political analysis, the New Testament itself would seem to be an excellent subject for such an exploration. For instance, a scholar of comparative politics may want to study the question of whether the political and religious institutions in place in Judea during the time of Jesus were essential to the rise of Christianity and its subsequent dominance of the Roman Empire. One of the first works of comparative politics in the early church is *The City of God* by St. Augustine of Hippo (A.D. 354-430). In that work, the great Christian theologian compares the heavenly city (the city of God) with the earthly city (the city of man), arguing that each has a different purpose.

AMERICAN POLITICS

American politics includes the study of America's political institutions, political parties, political movements, cultural practices, form of government, and the relationships between state, local, and federal governments and their many constituencies. A scholar of American politics may address these sorts of questions: Why did the Democratic Party win both houses of Congress in the 2006 midterm elections? Is there a relationship between personal income and party affiliation in the United States? Why did some evangelicals not vote Republican in the 2006 elections, as they did in 2004, 2002 and 2000? Is there a relationship between church attendance and party affiliation?

INTERNATIONAL RELATIONS (OR INTERNATIONAL AFFAIRS)

International relations is such a large and important field of study that some universities have schools and departments of international relations, studies or affairs that are not part of the same university's school or department of government, political science or politics. For example, Princeton University has a politics department along with the Woodrow Wilson School of Public and International Affairs.

Topics covered under international relations include international law, international human rights and the relationships between nation-states. Scholars may focus on specific questions such as the legitimacy and authority of international courts, the efficacy of the United Nations, the international enforceability of human rights declarations, the economic effect of tariffs on international trade, the statutory justification for war-crimes prosecution, and the causes and consequences of armed conflict between nations.

Christianity has been since its infancy a universal religion, one with global aspirations. Its founder and his early disciples did not think of their faith as limited by geography, ethnicity or nationalism. In the words of St. Paul, "There is neither Jew nor Greek, there is neither slave nor free man, there is neither male nor female; for you are all one in Christ Jesus" (Gal 3:28 NASB). The church that began with the Great Commission (Mt 28:16-20) has members from every nationality, ethnicity and virtually every language group. At the commencement of the twenty-first century, Christianity's future, many have argued,[7] lies in the world's southern hemisphere, far from the traditionally Christian West. Moreover, many scholars contend that the twentieth century's revolution in international human rights has its roots in the Judeo-Christian worldview, and that the human rights declarations that many of us rely on, secularists and believers alike, would not have arisen if not for the biblical understanding of human nature and intrinsic human dignity.[8] For these reasons, well-informed and philosophically sophisticated Christians have an important, and perhaps vital, role to play in the study and practice of international affairs.

---

[7]See Philip Jenkins, *The Next Christendom: The Coming of Global Christianity* (New York: Oxford University Press, 2002); and Philip Jenkins, *The New Faces of Christianity: Believing the Bible in the Global South* (New York: Oxford University Press, 2006).

[8]See Jerome J. Shestack, "The Jurisprudence of Human Rights," in *Human Rights in International Law: Legal and Policy Issues*, ed. Theodore Meron (Oxford: Clarendon, 1984), 1:69-113; John Warwick Montgomery, *Human Rights and Human Dignity* (Grand Rapids: Zondervan, 1986); George Weigel, *The Cube and the Cathedral: Europe, America and Politics Without God* (New York: Basic Books, 2005); and Louis P. Pojman, "A Critique of Contemporary Egalitarianism," *Faith and Philosophy* 8, no. 4 (October 1991): 481-506.

POLITICAL ECONOMY

Political economy involves the study of the relationship between politics and economics. A student in a political economy course will be exposed to different economic theories (e.g., Marxism, Keynsianism, classical, neoclassical, supply-side) and different economic systems (e.g., socialist, free market, mixed-economy) as well as critiques and defenses of all of them. Political economists also study the relationship between politics and economics, such as the question of how economic policy is influenced by political interest groups and vice versa.

Political economists have a variety of interests. Some of these include the questions of how wealth is created and what sorts of policies may inhibit or help facilitate economic growth. For example, suppose a political economist suggests that increasing the sales tax on yachts and private jets from 8 percent to 25 percent will only affect the wealthy (who can afford it) and will increase government revenues but allow a greater distribution of welfare payments to the poor. Imagine that this policy is implemented but the political economist's prediction does not come to pass. What happens is that the demand for luxury items decreases (since some of the "rich" are not "filthy rich"), the prices for these items are lowered in order to increase the demand, and the luxury-item manufacturers, distributors and retailers fire a large number of their workers since their employers can no longer afford their salaries. Moreover, those that benefited directly and indirectly from the sale and use of luxury items were harmed as well. For the tax increase resulted in decreasing sales of fuel, life vests, parachutes, cleaning articles, alcohol, first-aid kits, bait and tackle, and all sorts of other items. Yacht and private jet mechanics had less work, and thus less business and thus less income. So what the tax increase did was not "soak the rich," but paradoxically, it resulted in less tax revenue for the government, since it helped facilitate a decline in sales by artificially increasing the cost of the items, and because it created unemployed workers who no longer paid taxes and less prosperous businesses that paid fewer taxes.

Although one may agree with the many Christians who believe that the community has an obligation to help the poor in some way, a rudimentary understanding of political economy is essential. As is evident in the above example, good intentions to help the poor are not enough. One must understand, among other things, how wealth is created, how markets work, what sorts of government policies increase jobs and what type of monetary policy results in inflation (which hurts the poor since it increases the money supply while decreasing the value of that money, just as counterfeiting does when practiced by private individuals). And even if one were to master these aspects of political economy, it does not mean that one will know precisely what government policy is best. One also needs to have an understanding of human nature and what sorts of social institutions and practices make poverty less likely. For this reason, some political economists argue that the government should also be in the business of making sure that government policies do not undermine or interfere with certain institutions, practices and beliefs that flourish in economically prosperous communities, for example, intact families, an educated public, a commitment to the common good and a strong belief in the moral law.[9] It has been well documented,[10] for example, that the U.S. government's now-defunct (1935-1997) Aid to Families with Dependent Children (ADFC), though intended to provide financial help to single mothers below the poverty line, actually resulted in a dramatic increase in out-of-wedlock births. Because the government, according to ADFC critics, was literally paying women for having children out of wedlock, it got what it paid for. But it got more social pathologies and thus more poverty as well.[11] In 1996, President Bill Clinton, a Democrat, in cooperation with a Republican Congress, signed legislation that ended ADFC and replaced it with a program called Temporary Assistance for Needy Families (TANF). Although many critics of President Clinton's welfare reform in 1996 predicted dire consequences for the poor, in 2006 the liberal magazine *The New Republic* pointed out, "A broad consensus now holds that wel-

---

[9]See Jennifer Roback Morse, *Love and Economics: Why the Laissez-Faire Family Doesn't Work* (Dallas: Spence, 2001); and Robert P. George and Jean Bethke Elshtain, eds., *The Meaning of Marriage: Family, State, Market, and Morals* (Dallas: Spence, 2006).

[10]See Charles Murray, *Losing Ground: American Social Policy, 1950-1980*, 10th anniv. ed. (New York: Basic Books, 1994), pp. 124-34, 154-95.

[11]Ibid.

fare reform was certainly not a disaster—and that it may, in fact, have worked much as its designers had hoped."[12]

PUBLIC LAW

Public law concerns the areas of law that deal with the relationship between the government and individuals, both citizens and corporate entities: constitutional law, administrative law and criminal law. The institutions, branches and agencies of government are public entities that issue laws, regulations, ordinances and rules, and they have the absolute power to punish, tax, and coerce citizens and corporations, including businesses and churches. This is why it is called *public* law. In contrast, private law concerns the areas of law that deal with the relationship between private parties, such as the law of tort, property law and the law of contracts.

In the United States, constitutional law concerns the U.S. Constitution and its meaning on a variety of issues and cases. This includes questions having to do with the powers of the three branches of the federal government, the individual states and their relationship to each other. For example, the U.S. Congress cannot pass legislation that limits the powers of the executive branch (the President) explicitly mentioned in the Constitution. But if the president is the commander-in-chief, as the Constitution clearly states,[13] can Congress in any way limit his power to command the military other than exercising its power of the purse? Nobody knows for sure. Congress did pass the War Powers Act of 1973 (or War Powers Resolution),[14] which did in fact limit presidential power. There is debate as to whether this act is in fact constitutional.[15] Because no president has challenged the act, the Supreme Court has not weighed in on the matter.

Constitutional law also concerns matters of fundamental rights, those rights explicitly or (according to some) implicitly found in the Bill

---

[12]The Editors, "Fared Well," *The New Republic* 235, no. 10 (September 4, 2006): 7.

[13]U.S. Constitution, art. 2, sec. 2.

[14]*The War Powers Act of 1973*, Public Law 93-148, 50 U.S.C. 1541-1548.

[15]See Phillip Bobbitt, "War Powers: An Essay on John Hart Ely's *War and Responsibility: Constitutional Lessons of Vietnam and Its Aftermath*," *Michigan Law Quarterly* 92, no. 6 (May 1994): 1364-1400.

of Rights, the first ten amendments to the Constitution. Issues that touch on freedom of speech, religion, assembly and the right to privacy, as well those that concern criminal prosecution and property rights, are among the many that come under the rubric of "fundamental rights." This is why presidential appointments to the federal courts, including the U.S. Supreme Court, have taken on such importance in our political culture. Most of the issues that divide Americans—such as abortion, homosexuality, affirmative action and the proliferation of pornography—are ones that many Supreme Court justices have argued involve fundamental rights. Rights that are considered "fundamental" are rights the government cannot limit unless it has a really compelling reason to do so, such as limiting the freedom of speech by banning citizens from yelling "fire" in a crowded theater (if in fact there is no fire).[16] Of course, many citizens and jurists disagree, arguing that these matters and their regulation are best left to the individual states if one interprets the Constitution correctly. So, another aspect of studying constitutional law concerns constitutional interpretation and the different schools of thought that one finds among scholars and judges.

Administrative law concerns the sorts of statutes and rules that govern and give legislative, judicial and/or police powers to administrative agencies of local, state and federal governments, such as the Environmental Protection Agency (EPA), the Internal Revenue Service (IRS), the Department of Health and Human Services, The Gaming Control Board, Child Services, or the Division of Insurance. Administrative agencies may investigate, prosecute and punish citizens. So, for example, the IRS, which is a bureau of the Treasury Department (which is part of the federal executive branch) has within its authority the power to enact general laws called "revenue rulings" (a legislative function), prosecute tax cheats (an executive function), issue opinions to individuals (such as "private letter rulings") and punish lawbreakers by fining them (quasi-judicial functions).

Most people are familiar with criminal law because of its promi-

---

[16]This comes from a famous line by Justice Oliver Wendell Holmes Jr., "The most stringent protection of free speech would not protect a man in falsely shouting fire in a theater and causing a panic" (*Schenck v. United States*, 249 U.S. 47, 52 [1919]).

nence in popular books, movies and television programs, not to mention the famous court cases involving celebrities, captains of industry and ordinary people who are accused of committing particularly heinous acts (e.g., the Scott Peterson case). This area of public law involves the state's authority and power to prosecute wrongs and punish citizens who commit these wrongs. This is why criminal cases have names such as *The People v. O. J. Simpson*, for it is the state, and not a private individual, that is bringing action against a defendant.

As one would suspect, these areas of public law overlap. For example, the Supreme Court, in the case of *Mapp v. Ohio* (1961),[17] and again in the more famous case of *Miranda v. Arizona* (1966),[18] affirmed an application of the Constitution's Fourth Amendment[19] that is known in criminal law as the exclusionary rule: evidence acquired illegally cannot be used in a criminal case against a defendant. Here we have criminal law and constitutional law overlapping.

CONCLUSION

In this chapter we covered the study of politics by briefly perusing six of its subfields: political theory, comparative politics, American politics, international relations, political economy and public law. Although these subfields are presented here in isolation of one another, they cannot help but intersect on many issues and questions. For example, in the study of the global economy and its differing effects on various political systems, one will likely consult scholars in comparative politics, political economy and international affairs. And if one wants to assess the fairness or justice of these effects, one will have to appeal to principles of a political theory that give one warrant for this assessment. And sup-

---

[17]*Mapp v. Ohio*, 367 U.S. 643 (1961).

[18]*Miranda v. Arizona*, 384 U.S. 436 (1966). Chief Justice Earl Warren wrote in the Court's opinion, "The prosecution may not use statements, whether exculpatory or inculpatory, stemming from questioning initiated by law enforcement officers after a person has been taken into custody or otherwise deprived of his freedom of action in any significant way, unless it demonstrates the use of procedural safeguards effective to secure the Fifth Amendment's privilege against self-incrimination."

[19]"The right of the people to be secure in their persons, houses, papers, and effects, against unreasonable searches and seizures, shall not be violated, and no Warrants shall issue, but upon probable cause, supported by Oath or affirmation, and particularly describing the place to be searched, and the persons or things to be seized." U.S. Constitution, amend. 4.

pose the United States, in its participation with the global economy, signs agreements with other nations that seem to require the United States to violate the Endangered Species Act, which is enforced by the Environmental Protection Agency. In order to evaluate this claim, one must confer with scholarship in public law (in particular, administrative and constitutional law).

These subfields, as I have already noted, do not even come close to exhausting the field of politics. Nevertheless, our brief overview of them provides the Christian student with an introductory understanding of what sorts of areas he may find of interest. It also offers the student an opportunity to explore within these subfields issues and debates that should be of concern for the Christian citizen, even if she is not interested in politics as an academic subject. This brings us to our next topic, liberal democracy and the Christian citizen, which is the focus of chapter two.

LIBERAL DEMOCRACY
AND THE CHRISTIAN CITIZEN

What does it mean to be a Christian citizen in a liberal democracy in the early twenty-first century? Most citizens, including most Christian citizens, in North America and Europe will tell you without batting an eye that liberal democracy is the best form of government. However, these same citizens often have a difficult time explaining what liberal democracy is and what would justify a Christian contribution to it.

Liberal democracies have been absent from most of history, and thus most of Christian history as well. However, Christians have largely embraced liberal democracy, for four primary reasons: (1) it affords them the liberty to worship, (2) it protects the people's power to hold the government accountable, (3) it allows citizens to participate by voting, forming political parties and coalitions, running for office, and/or campaigning for causes and candidates, and (4) it seems consistent with and supported by a Christian understanding of the human person as well as the natural law and natural-rights traditions that spring from that understanding.

In this chapter, I will address reasons 1-3 by showing how liberal democracy relates to the Christian worldview. I will accomplish this by offering first an explanation of liberal democracy and the separation-of-powers version of it, and second, an account of what it means to be a Christian citizen. I will not deal with reason 4 in this chapter, for it will be the focus of chapter five.

LIBERAL DEMOCRACY AND THE SEPARATION OF POWERS

The *liberal* part of *liberal democracy* refers to the liberties or freedoms the government is supposed to guarantee. These include freedom of religion, speech, assembly and press, as well as the right to own property. The *democracy* part of *liberal democracy* refers to at least two principles: self-governance and equality of citizens before the law. *Self-governance* means a representative government that is ultimately accountable to the people. To say that citizens ought to be equal before the law means that the laws must be applied fairly and justly, that all similarly situated citizens must be treated similarly. So, for instance, if citizen Jones, a blue-collar worker, is arrested for stealing $100, he should be accorded the same rights to due process, a jury trial and legal representation as Smith, a Microsoft executive, who was indicted for embezzling a million dollars.

But in order for liberal democracy to work well, the nation must be under the rule of law and have a developed civil society. The rule of law means that there are legal instruments (or documents), such as a constitution or a charter, that clearly present and limit the powers of the government's branches, outline the people's rights and privileges, and explain how laws are passed, changed or eliminated. This rule of law, and not the rule of capricious and arbitrary leaders, is the structure under which the government governs and the people's rights are protected. For this reason, a liberal democracy cannot be a pure democracy, one in which everything is voted on directly by the people. This would degenerate into mob rule and would be inadequate to protect the rights of minorities or citizens that hold unpopular beliefs. So, paradoxically, in order for liberal democracy to work well, there must be unassailable first principles that the government or even a majority cannot be free to change. Thus, both the power of the people and the powers of the different branches of government ought to be constitutionally limited.

Liberal democracy also requires a civil society—a community that consists of numerous overlapping institutions, such as families, religious bodies (e.g., churches), schools, professional associations, labor unions, fraternal organizations, etc., that provide places in which the moral requirements of citizenship may be nurtured and by which citizens may express themselves. That is, nongovernment institutions do most of the work in civilizing a nation's people by shaping its character. Consequently, without a civil society that respects the rule of law and teaches its future generations to respect it as well, even the most well-written constitution will not result in a just regime. But the reverse is also true; the government may for good or ill affect the development of civil society. For example, some have argued that the pervasiveness of no-fault divorce has had negative consequences on the institution of the family.[1]

Different societies have devised a variety of ways to preserve and protect the principles of liberal democracy. One approach is to institute a government structure that is a separation of powers. The government of the United States is an example of this type of government.

The United States is sometimes called a constitutional republic of separated powers. A republic is a nation that is based on the consent of the governed as well as the principles of liberal democracy articulated above. Thus, to say that the United States is a constitutional republic means that it is a nation whose government is based on an authoritative document, the Constitution, in which the government's powers and the rights of its people are enumerated so that it may govern—pass and enforce laws and judge disputes between citizens and between citizens and the state—in accordance with principles and rules known to all parties through the Constitution.

By *separation of powers*, I mean that each government of the United States (whether federal, state or local) and each branch of those governments (whether executive, legislative or judicial) has its own scope of authority and powers unique to itself. When each exercises its authority and powers, sometimes in conflict with the interests and views of the others (e.g., the President vetoes a piece of legislation passed by majorities in both houses of Congress), a compromise is likely to occur if any side hopes to have its views and the interests of its constituency even partially reflected in the laws. This places limits on governments and reduces the likelihood of tyranny and despotism.

---

[1]See Jennifer Roback Morse's essay, "Why Unilateral Divorce Has No Place in a Free Society," in *The Meaning of Marriage: Family, State, Market, and Morals*, ed. Robert P. George and Jean Bethke Elshtain (Dallas: Spence, 2006), pp. 74-99.

From the very beginning and through most of its history, two parties have dominated American electoral politics. The first two major parties were the Democrat-Republican Party (the predecessor of today's Democratic Party) and the Federalist Party. Today, the parties are Republican and Democrat, each holding to (officially, in the party platforms) contrary points of view on a variety of issues that are important to Christians, such as the moral status of the unborn, gay rights, public education, constitutional interpretation, judicial appointments, and the relationship between religion and government. There are, of course, recalcitrant members in each party, largely because of the demographics and cultural histories of the geographical regions in which they were elected. So, one finds the phenomena of the "liberal Republican" (e.g., former New York City mayor, Rudolph Giuliani) in the Northeast and the "conservative Democrat" in the South (e.g., former Georgia U.S. Senator Zel Miller).

Nevertheless, in legislative bodies the majority party is essentially in control of the sort of legislation that makes it to the floor for a final vote. This is because the majority party controls the leadership of the legislative body, including the chairmanships of committees that decide what legislation can get out of committee to then be debated and voted on by the entire body. So, if party X has a platform that affirms abortion rights, and party X is the majority party in the U.S. Senate, party X's policy preferences on abortion will be advanced even if a few members of that party who are U.S. senators are not supporters of abortion rights.

Of course, many liberal democracies do not have a U.S.-type separation of powers. Most, however, have mechanisms in place that are intended to preserve and protect the principles of liberal democracy. For example, the United Kingdom has what is sometimes called a "fusion of powers," since the different branches of government have their source in the legislature (i.e., Parliament). In the United Kingdom the executive branch, the office of prime minister, is created by Parliament when the monarch appoints a member of the ruling party of the House of Commons (and very rarely, the House of Lords) to be the nation's executive. The prime minister then makes cabinet appointments, selecting Parliament members from his or her own political party. Despite having a Parliament as the source of all government branches, the U.K. government does contains checks and balances, though certainly not identical to what is found in the United States. This is also true of other liberal democracies that have less separation of powers than the United States.

THE CHRISTIAN CITIZEN

Although the New Testament speaks very little about government and the Christian's responsibility as a citizen, one may glean certain principles from the Bible that contribute to understanding why a Christian citizen should have an interest in politics and political institutions.

In order to accomplish this goal, we will cover four topics (1) Caesar's coin and the image of God, (2) doing justice, (3) knowing your government, its laws and the scope of your citizenship, and (4) voting for and supporting non-Christian candidates. Because each of these topics can be addressed individually in a book-length treatment, we can only hope to skim the surface of each one here. In addressing these topics, my goal is not to propose what I think is the correct Christian perspective on politics, but rather, to offer the reader some biblical and theological ways to think about politics and the role of the Christian citizen in a liberal democracy.

CAESAR'S COIN AND THE IMAGE OF GOD

In a familiar scene, the Pharisees confront Jesus with an apparent dilemma:

> "Tell us, then, what is your opinion: Is it lawful to pay the census tax to Caesar or not?" Knowing their malice, Jesus said, "Why are you testing me, you hypocrites? Show me the coin that pays the census tax." Then they handed him the Roman coin. He said to them, "Whose image is this and whose inscription?" They replied, "Caesar's." At that he said to them, "Then repay to Caesar what belongs to Caesar and to God what belongs to God." When they heard this they were amazed, and leaving him they went away. (Mt 22:17-22 NAB)

The most dominant reading of this passage is that Jesus is instructing his audience that the church and government have jurisdiction over different spheres of authority. Although I believe this reading is largely correct, those who present it often miss the subtle political implications of what Jesus says. He first asks whose image is on the coin. The answer, of course, is Caesar's. But an unsaid question begs an answer: What (or who) has the image of God on it?[2] That is, if the coin represents the authority of Caesar because it has his image on it, then we, human beings, are under the authority of God because we have his image on us. And all governments are not only comprised of human beings, but the governments themselves are imbued with responsibility for the human beings under their power. Good governments ought to be concerned with the well-being of their citizens and these citizens correctly believe that their well-being is best sustained by a just government. Thus, both government and the church, though having separate jurisdictions, share a common obligation to advance the good of those who are made in God's image.

This implies not only that we should not confuse the state and the church, but it also implies that we should be concerned with those who have the image of God on them, our fellow human beings. This concern may be expressed in a number of different ways. We can help the poor, feed the hungry, clothe the naked or comfort the afflicted. This can be accomplished by our churches or by the wider community through government programs. The issue for Christians is not whether one should support works of mercy and charity. We are commanded to do so by the Scriptures (Mt 25:31-46; Jas 1:26-27). Rather, the real question is, what is the best way to achieve success in these endeavors? Christians in nations that have a strong history of religious liberty and the separation of church and state are divided on this question. Some, such as Marvin Olasky,[3] emphasize free-market solutions, with government playing a minimal role and the church doing virtually all of

---

[2]This is an insight I learned from Luis Lugo in his essay "Caesar's Coin and the Politics of the Kingdom: A Pluralist Perspective," in *Caesar's Coin Revisited: Christians the Limits of Government*, ed. Michael Cromartie (Grand Rapids: Eerdmans, 1996), pp. 14-15.
[3]See Marvin Olasky, *The Tragedy of American Compassion* (Chicago: Regnery, 1992).

the work. Others, such as Jim Wallis,[4] maintain that some social welfare programs administered by the government are necessary, and they call for churches to participate in helping the poor by both politically advocating government programs and doing their own independent work. Many in both camps have advocated a type of compromise in which the government and churches cooperate to fund and administer certain programs. These usually come under the heading of "faith-based initiatives."[5] In fact, the Department of Commerce has a Center for Faith-Based and Neighborhood Partnerships that offers financial and technical assistance to interested groups.[6] However, still other Christians have raised questions about whether such cooperation—which involves the distribution of tax dollars to churches and church-affiliated organizations—may violate America's longstanding tradition of church-state separation.[7] (The meaning of church-state separation is the subject of the next chapter, chapter 3.) Because faith-based organizations that receive government funding cannot use these monies for inherently religious activities including proselytizing, some Christians have argued that such restrictions limit the spiritual resources that a ministry may access while administering their services. Others have suggested that it is nearly impossible to sequester a ministry's evangelistic mission from its works of charity and mercy, since the ministry's theology often informs and guides all its tasks. For this reason, the government's restrictions can be difficult to follow in actual practice.

Yet another consideration for this discussion is the Christian theological understanding of charity works: their purpose is not merely to help the poor and others who need the church's love and care, but also to allow the grace of God to work through individuals and communi-

---

[4]Jim Wallis, *God's Politics: Why the Right Gets It Wrong and the Left Doesn't Get It* (San Francisco: HarperCollins, 2005).

[5]See Center for Public Justice, *Guide to Charitable Choice* (Washington, D.C.: Center for Public Justice, 1997). Produced in conjunction with Center for Law & Religious Freedom of the Christian Legal Society.

[6]Center for Faith-Based and Neighborhood Partnerships <www.commerce.gov/OS/CFBCI/index.htm>.

[7]See, for example, Charles McDaniel, Derek H. Davis and Sabrina Neff, "Charitable Choice and Prison Ministries: Constitutional and Institutional Challenges to Rehabilitating the American Penal System," *Criminal Justice Policy Review* 16, no. 2 (2005): 164-89.

ties so that they can be conformed to the image of Christ and bear witness to the world of God's grace. According to Jesus (Mt 7:12-27), it is the bearing of fruit, the hearing and acting on Christ's words, and doing the will of his father that constitute the life of faith—a life likened by Jesus to a house that could fall if not adequately constructed to withstand severe adversity. In John 14, Jesus gives his followers a glimpse of what this kind of connection means when he says, "because I live, you will live also" (Jn 14:19 NKJV). He states, "At that day you will know that I *am* in my Father, and you in me, and I in you. He who has My commandments and keeps them, it is he who loves Me; and he who loves Me will be loved by My Father, and I will love him and manifest Myself to him" (Jn 14:20-21 NKJV). And these commandments include "love your neighbor as yourself" (Mk 12:28-31 NIV) and the acts of love that the goats lacked at the Last Judgment (Mt 25:31-46). The Gospel of Mark recounts these words of Christ, "If any man would come after him, let him deny himself, and take up his cross, and follow me. For whosoever would save his life shall lose it; and whoever loses his life for my sake and the gospel's shall save it" (Mk 8:34-35 ASV). In Mark 4, Jesus explains the parable of the seeds, telling of those who receive the word "with joy," but it does not take root and thus they fall away immediately "when trouble or persecution comes" (Mk 4:16-17 NIV). He also tells of "the ones sown on good soil," who "hear the word and accept it and produce a crop—thirty, sixty, or even a hundred times what was sown" (Mk 4:20 NIV). It seems then that the Christian gospel is as much about getting heaven into people as about getting people into heaven. Thus, the Christian should not be too quick to accept government solutions that may have the unintended consequence of impeding the church's opportunity to bear witness to Christ's grace in their works of charity and mercy.

Among those who are made in the image of God are children. If Jesus commands everyone to give "unto God what is God's," followers of Christ must, therefore, ask themselves what sorts of policies, practices and institutions best advance the good of the nation's youth. Unfortunately, there are those in contemporary culture who look at children as merely products of choice and value them to whatever extent they may bring happiness to the adults who desire them.[8] But this objectifies children and does not seem consistent with the biblical tradition, which portrays children as begotten, not made, and as gifts from God rather than products of our wills (Ps 127:3). This is not to say that one must be a Christian to hold such a high view of human dignity, for many non-Christian citizens, both religious and non-religious, hold such a view. These citizens, like their Christian peers, see children as persons that should be valued for their own sake rather than because of what children can do for others. Thus, the objectification of children should trouble both Christians and non-Christians alike.

A proper understanding of children and the obligations that adults have to them are essential to a well-ordered society. As Jesus pointed out, "Is there anyone among you who, if your child asks for a fish, will give a snake instead of a fish? Or if the child asks for an egg, will give a scorpion? If you then, who are evil, know how to give good gifts to your children, how much more will the heavenly Father give the Holy Spirit to those who ask him!" (Lk 11:11-13 NRSV). And because our neighbor's child is our neighbor as well, and we should love our neighbor as ourselves (Mt 22:39), many Christians think it wise, through laws and cultural practices, to protect the institutions of marriage and the family. For those institutions, when healthy, are more likely to produce well-adjusted children who become good citizens and thus contribute to the common good. So Christians in a liberal democracy, because they have the means to effect change, should be concerned about whether the wider culture and/or their government agencies and institutions (such as the public schools) are properly shaping, or at least not corrupting, the character of its young people.

DOING JUSTICE

Using language that assumes the universality of human responsibilities across times and cultures, the Scriptures instruct the state, the individual and intermediate institutions to do justice. Christ, for example,

---

[8]See, for example, John A. Robertson, *Children of Choice: Freedom and the New Reproductive Technologies* (Princeton, N.J.: Princeton University Press, 1994).

tells us to love our neighbors as ourselves (Lk 10:27), and offers the parable of the Good Samaritan in order to help us understand that the stranger too is our neighbor and entitled to be treated justly (Lk 10:29-37). The Old Testament abounds with calls for justice and condemnations of injustice (e.g., Deut 24:19-22; Prov 31:8-9; Is 58:6-10). The Ten Commandments (Ex 20:2-17) reveal something of God's plan for a rightly ordered, or socially just, community. We are to worship God, honor our mothers and fathers, remain faithful to our spouses, not covet or steal our neighbors' property or spouse, maintain integrity in word and deed, and respect the intrinsic dignity of human life. In present-day political terms this can translate to the government respecting and privileging religious liberty, the right to life, private property, traditional marriage, male-female parenthood and integrity in public life.

The first crime recorded in the Bible is Cain's murder of Abel (Gen 4:1-16), even though there was no written law to speak of at the time. This means that one can know justice and injustice apart from governments or written law; knowledge of the moral law does not depend on acquaintance with any external earthly authority. For it is by the moral law that we judge governments and written laws as either just or unjust. That is why God could legitimately hold Cain accountable for his crime even though there were no criminal statutes at the time.

Because many Christians reside in liberal democracies in which citizens play an integral part in electing their leaders, shaping policy and enforcing laws, these governments allow Christians to do justice at a level of participation their brethren in the ancient and medieval church would have considered unthinkable. What this justice constitutes, and how best to go about implementing it, is the subject of great debate among Christians. For example, as I noted above, all Christians agree that we have an obligation to help the poor. Some support a strong welfare system, while others believe that such a system may sometimes work to harm the poor and their future prospects.

A Christian's moral obligation to do justice may also involve concern for the public culture and how it affects the virtue of its citizens. Political theorist Robert P. George refers to this as a community's "moral ecology."[9] We know that film, art, television, literature, the Internet, and other forms of entertainment and expression have the power to shape and influence a culture. This is why businesses advertise: it works! They know very well that a well-crafted image or a string of carefully fashioned words has the power to change minds and hearts. This should not surprise us. Jesus uttered parables, not doctrinal treatises, in order to teach theological truths, just as Plato penned his entertaining dialogues in order to offer philosophical arguments on an array of issues concerning the nature of knowledge, reality, politics and law. Everyone knows the story of the Good Samaritan, but virtually no one, except for a handful of professors, can recite to you the version of Immanuel Kant's categorical imperative they were taught in college. Stories and images matter.

Just as the natural environment of Earth requires an ecological balance, so does the moral environment of a culture. Just as a polluted river has the potential to negatively impact fish, wildlife, recreation and industry, a polluted culture can impair the moral ecology of a community. This seems uncontroversial. There is no doubt, for example, that the relentless teaching of anti-Semitism in Islamic schools in the Middle East, and its importation to American mosques, has had a profound effect in shaping Muslim attitudes toward the state of Israel and the Jewish people.[10] Thus, it is not surprising that in the United States some of the fiercest political and legal battles are over public school curricula. Activists from many sides clash over the content of everything from sex education courses to the teaching of evolution in science classes. For all sides know that ideas have consequences and that whoever controls what and how ideas are communicated in the schools shapes the beliefs of the next generation. This holds no less true for other cultural phenomena including the assorted media that incessantly bombard people from all angles, such as radio, television, film and the Internet. Consequently, if

---

[9]Robert P. George, *Making Men Moral: Civil Liberties and Public Morality* (New York: Oxford University Press, 1992), p. 46.

[10]See Freedom House, *Saudi Publications on Hate Ideology Fill American Mosques* (Washington, D.C.: Center for Religious Freedom, 2005); Amon Groiss, ed., *The West, Christians and Jews in Saudi Arabian Schoolbooks* (New York: Center for Monitoring the Impact of Peace and the American Jewish Committee, 2003).

a Christian truly endeavors to love her neighbor as herself, she should be just as worried about her neighbor's loss of virtue—resulting from, and contributing to, an imbalance in her community's moral ecology—as she is with the loss of her neighbor's physical health caused by, for example, an excess of automobile emissions. Of course, Christians will disagree on how best to address this concern.

And yet, the Christian must exercise care in the extent to which the government uses its power to protect a community's moral ecology. Take, for example, the debate over gay rights. There is a wide range of opinion on this subject, even among Christians. Very few (if any) Christians, even very conservatives ones, argue for the state to criminalize homosexual behavior that takes place in private between consenting adults, though most Christians would not argue that homosexual practice is good or ought to be celebrated by the state. Others defend not only these privacy rights, but also support laws that protect gays from employment and housing discrimination.[11] And some liberal Christians go even further and defend the legalization of same-sex marriage.[12] And yet it is clear to the Catholic and Orthodox churches and virtually all evangelical Protestant scholars that a society that embraces same-sex marriage has effectively abandoned a fundamental truth about human beings—marriage is a one-flesh communion between one man and one woman[13]—supported by both Scripture and natural law that is essential for the common good.[14]

A Christian must be prudent and wise about how he or she addresses the volatile issues that arise out of the debate over gay rights. First, he must never forget that homosexuals—even if he believes that homo-

---

[11]See Tony Campolo, "Gains for the Democrats Among Evangelicals," *The Huffington Post*, April 28, 2008 <www.huffingtonpost.com/tony-campolo/gains-for-the-democrats-a_b_99089.html>.

[12]Marvin M. Ellison, "Should the Traditional Understanding of Marriage as the One-Flesh Union of a Man and a Woman Be Abandoned?" *Philosophia Christi* 7 (2005): 7-13; Ronald E. Long, "In Support of Same-Sex Marriage," *Philosophia Christi* 7 (2005): 29-39.

[13]Of course, violations of this understanding are rampant among heterosexuals as evidenced by the wide acceptance of extramarital sex (both before and after marriage) and no-fault divorce.

[14]See Robert P. George and Jean Bethke Elshtain, *The Meaning of Marriage: Family, State, Market, and Morals* (Dallas: Spence, 2006); and Robert A. J. Gagnon, *The Bible and Homosexual Practice: Texts and Hermeneutics* (Nashville: Abingdon, 2001).

sexual behavior is immoral and harmful to those who practice it (as many Christians, including me, believe)—are persons made in the image of God. Thus Christians must not allow their support of the sanctity of marriage to obstruct their love toward those for whom Christ died, including homosexual neighbors and friends. For this reason, Christians should focus on what they support rather than merely on what they oppose, though at times they cannot avoid speaking frankly about what they believe about human sexuality and the nature of marriage. When disagreements arise, Christians should ask dissenting friends and neighbors to extend to them the tolerance and open-mindedness those who disagree often (and I believe, inaccurately) claim that Christians lack.

Second, because Christians, even in the United States, live in widely different communities, one has to be realistic about what one can achieve by the political process. In some locales, the best a Christian can do is make an effort to protect the church from being coerced by the state to violate Christian moral theology. In Massachusetts, for example, soon after the state's supreme judicial court in 2003 required that the state issue marriage licenses to same-sex couples,[15] Catholic Charities, which was at the time in the child adoption business, was told by the state that it could no longer exclude same-sex couples as adoptee parents, even though the Catholic Church maintains that same-sex unions are deeply disordered and sinful. Because it did not want to compromise its moral theology, Catholic Charities, sadly, ceased offering children for adoption.[16] Even if one supports gay rights, this forced departure of Christian kindness from the public square is an appalling violation of religious liberty. It means that a religious organization with an outstanding track record in placing children in loving homes had to stop that activity simply because it would not acquiesce to the state's requirement that it abandon its theological understanding of the nature of marriage and family. It seems to me that, in situations like this, Christians have a right to

---

[15] *Goodridge v. Dept. of Public Health*, 440 Mass. 309 (2003).
[16] Maggie Gallagher, "Banned in Boston," *The Weekly Standard*, May 16, 2006 <www.weekly standard.com/Content/Public/Articles/000/000/012/191kgwgh.asp>.

resist such an intrusion by the state on the practice of the church's moral theology.

For this reason, Christian citizens should know that laws and court opinions defended as liberating for one group may in practice nurture cultural and political hostility toward Christians and citizens from other religious traditions. Political philosopher Hadley Arkes points out that a legal regime that endorses same-sex unions sets into motion a certain moral logic that will likely result in the condemnation and marginalization of those, especially traditional Christians and Jews, who resist this endorsement in their communities and institutions. For example (this is my example, not Arkes's), a philosophy department at an evangelical Christian college that receives federal funds yet refuses to hire "married" same-sex couples, may, according to this moral logic, have its government funding withdrawn for engaging in unlawful discrimination based on marital status. For this reason, Arkes refers to one congressional bill that would have banned discrimination against homosexuals by private businesses,[17] as the "Christian and Jewish Removal Act," "for it promises to purge serious Christians and Jews from the executive suites of corporations, universities, and law firms."[18] After all, why would a university hire a Christian philosophy professor who holds "discriminatory" views if the espousal of such views could put the school at risk of civil or criminal litigation? For such a faculty member, if hired, would serve on search committees and be involved with hirings and promotions in a variety of ways. And if any gays or lesbians were to be rejected by the committee on which this faculty member served, his or her views could be cited as evidence of discrimination if the rejected applicant were to file a lawsuit. This is not at all far fetched. Arkes, for example, tells of the case of "the wife of a shop owner in Boulder, Colorado [who] had given a pamphlet on homosexuality to a gay employee. For that offense, she was charged under the local ordinance on gay rights, and compelled to enter a program of compulsory

---

[17]For more on the "Employment Non-Discrimination Act" or ENDA, see <http://community .pflag.org/Page.aspx?pid=448>.

[18]Hadley Arkes, "Homosexuality and the Law," in *Homosexuality and American Public Life*, ed. Christopher Wolfe (Dallas: Spence, 1999), p. 165.

counseling."[19] Because politics, like nature, abhors a vacuum, these sorts of stories of religious bigotry and discrimination of Christians and other religious citizens have become increasingly common since Arkes related this story in 1996. After all, a government that stipulates that a negative moral judgment of homosexual conduct is akin to racism or other forms of invidious discrimination will not, for long, remain tolerant of those who, for reasons of honest and careful moral reflection, sincerely dissent from what they see as an inflexible and coercive state-mandated orthodoxy.

Knowing Your Government, Its Laws and the Scope of Your Citizenship

The Scriptures seem to teach that people have an obligation to understand the nature of their government and its laws, and employ that knowledge so that the gospel is not disadvantaged by the state. According to St. Paul, Christians ought to obey generally applicable laws because they receive their authority from God. Thus, to disobey such laws is tantamount to disobeying God. Writes St. Paul:

> Obey the rulers who have authority over you. Only God can give authority to anyone, and he puts these rulers in their places of power. People who oppose the authorities are opposing what God has done, and they will be punished. Rulers are a threat to evil people, not to good people. There is no need to be afraid of the authorities. Just do right, and they will praise you for it.
>
> After all, they are God's servants, and it is their duty to help you. If you do something wrong, you ought to be afraid, because these rulers have the right to punish you. They are God's servants who punish criminals to show how angry God is. But you should obey the rulers because you know it is the right thing to do, and not just because of God's anger.
>
> You must also pay your taxes. The authorities are God's servants, and it is their duty to take care of these matters. Pay all that you owe, whether it is taxes and fees or respect and honor. (Romans 13:1-7 CEV)

In order to comply with St. Paul's instructions, citizens must be con-

---

[19]Hadley Arkes, "A Culture Corrupted," *First Things* 67 (November 1996) <www.firstthings.com/ftissues/ft9611/articles/arkes.html>.

versant with the laws of their government and the rules and regulations they are required to obey. The apostle also rejects a consequentialist justification for this obedience. That is, he urges his readers to obey the law, not merely because they will be punished if they don't, but rather, because "it is the right thing to do"—even if they know that they won't be punished if they disobey.

However, it would be a mistake to take the apostle's general advice to the Romans and apply it to situations in which a good law is administered unjustly and/or the government punishes the good and rewards evil or when the authorities instruct Christian citizens to betray the principles of the gospel.

Concerning the case of unjustly administered law, the book of Acts records an incident in which St. Paul, after being beaten and imprisoned with Silas for preaching the gospel, appeals to his Roman citizenship in order to exercise his civil rights and to remedy a wrong:

> But when it was day, the magistrates sent the lictors [the Roman magistrates' attendees] with the order, "Release those men." The jailer reported the[se] words to Paul, "The magistrates have sent orders that you be released. Now, then, come out and go in peace." But Paul said to them, "They have beaten us publicly, even though we are Roman citizens and have not been tried, and have thrown us into prison. And now, are they going to release us secretly? By no means. Let them come themselves and lead us out." The lictors reported these words to the magistrates, and they became alarmed when they heard that they were Roman citizens. So they came and placated them, and led them out and asked that they leave the city. (Acts 16:35-38 NAB)

Several points stand out here. (1) The apostle used political status—Roman citizenship—in order to ensure that the gospel could be preached freely. (2) St. Paul was not afraid to exercise the rights that this political status accorded him as an act of community leadership, even if it struck fear in the hearts of the magistrates. (3) He directly cited a violation of his rights as a citizen—lack of due process ("we . . . have not been tried")—against those in the government that committed the act. (4) St. Paul employed political leverage to correct an injustice done to him and a fellow Christian.

Today, citizenship, especially in liberal democracies, carries with it a greater array of rights and responsibilities than the apostle Paul ever had. Thus, if St. Paul saw nothing tawdry or un-Christian about employing his Roman citizenship, and the rights and powers that accompanied it, in order to protect the gospel and to remedy a wrong, then Christians ought to take their own citizenship just as seriously when the proper time and circumstance requires them to avail themselves of its powers.

The book of Acts also records another sort of encounter between the church and the civil authorities (Acts 5:17-42). This situation concerned the right of Christian believers to preach the gospel. The apostles were imprisoned in a public jail by the Jewish Sadducee high priest and his colleagues. After an angel released the apostles that evening, the Sadducees convened the council of Jewish authorities and requested that the apostles be brought before it. But the apostles were not in jail any longer; they were in the temple preaching the gospel. When the council members heard this, the captain of the temple guards and his men went to the temple and escorted the apostles back to the council. The text then records the following exchange:

> When they had brought them, they stood them [the apostles] before the Council. The high priest questioned them, saying, "We gave you strict orders not to continue teaching in this name, and yet, you have filled Jerusalem with your teaching and intend to bring this man's blood upon us." But Peter and the apostles answered, "We must obey God rather than men. The God of our fathers raised up Jesus, whom you had put to death by hanging Him on a cross. He is the one whom God exalted to His right hand as a Prince and a Savior, to grant repentance to Israel, and forgiveness of sins.
>
> "And we are witnesses of these things; and *so is* the Holy Spirit, whom God has given to those who obey Him." (Acts 5:27-32 NASB)

In this case, the infant church disobeyed the civil authorities because they were requiring that the church not obey Christ's command to preach the gospel (Mt 28:19-20). This records a clear case of a political regime oppressing the church. But it also reveals a posture biblical commentators often miss: the apostles had an incredibly high view of the truth-value of the message they were preaching. Rather than appealing to a "right to conscience" or some modern concept of religious liberty to justify their preaching (though there is certainly nothing wrong in appealing to such concepts), the apostles told the high priest that they were justified in preaching the gospel because they had good reason to believe that the gospel was true. Given the religious nature of the civil authority they were encountering—a Jewish council—the apostles delivered to that body the only sort of argument that could justify what they were doing in the minds of their oppressors: "We have knowledge of a truth that gives us the warrant, and thus authority, to do what we are doing." Of course, the council members were not persuaded by the apostles' argument, for "they, when they heard this, were cut to the heart, and minded to slay them [the apostles]" (Acts 5:33 asv).

It took the intervention and clever rhetoric of the Pharisee Gamaliel, a doctor of the law, to convince the council to accept, in principle, the apostles' argument, without the council actually realizing it. Gamaliel maintained that if the apostles were correct about Jesus, then preventing them from preaching the gospel would put the council in the position of fighting God. On the other hand, if the apostles were mistaken about Jesus, then they would go the way of other followers of would-be messiahs who quickly vanished from the scene (Acts 5:34-40). After giving them a beating and telling them to stop speaking in the name of Jesus, the council let the apostles go free. The apostles of course continued to preach the gospel after they departed the council's presence, and counted their suffering for Christ as a badge of honor (Acts 5:40-42).

This story teaches more than the obvious lesson that Christians may at times be obligated to disobey the civil authorities, just as Hebrew midwives disobeyed Pharaoh's command to kill all newborn boys (Ex 1:17). It also teaches that Christians may legitimately appeal to being justified in knowing their beliefs to be true in order to defend their place and actions in the polity.

This is significant because too often in our contemporary culture, theologically informed beliefs are not considered a legitimate claim to knowledge. This is why, for example, it is enough for some commentators to call a belief "religious" in order to treat it as an item that cannot be reflected in our laws or be part of our political regime. For we would consider it strange if someone dismissed another's political views because they were judged by lawyers, politicians and editorialists as "history," "science" or "journalism." If an idea is labeled "religious," it is essentially being called nonsense. This understanding is so much a part of our public culture that many people think nothing of it when it is presented to us in policy discussions.

Take, for example, the 2004 speech given by Ron Reagan,[20] the son of the late U.S. President Ronald W. Reagan.[21] Commenting on Americans who oppose embryonic stem-cell research, the younger Reagan argued:

> Now, there are those who would stand in the way of this remarkable future, who would deny the federal funding so crucial to basic research. They argue that interfering with the development of even the earliest stage embryo, even one that will never be implanted in a womb and will never develop into an actual fetus, is tantamount to murder. . . . [M]any are well-meaning and sincere. Their belief is just that, an article of faith, and they are entitled to it.
>
> But it does not follow that the theology of a few should be allowed to forestall the health and well-being of the many. And how can we affirm life if we abandon those whose own lives are so desperately at risk?[22]

For the younger Reagan, one's theological tradition can never in principle trump the goals of "health" and "well-being." Perhaps realizing that these terms and their meanings cannot be understood and known apart from more fundamental beliefs about human beings and their nature, Reagan offers an account of the value of nascent life that sequesters early embryos from the class of moral subjects. He maintains that early embryos "are not, in and of themselves, human beings,"[23]

---

[20]This paragraph and the following five paragraphs (including the two from Reagan) are adapted from pages 458-61 of my article "Taking Theology Seriously: The Status of the Religious Beliefs of Judicial Nominees for the Federal Bench," *Notre Dame Journal of Law, Ethics, & Public Policy* 20, no. 1 (2006): 455-71.

[21]Ron Reagan, "Ron Reagan's Remarks at the Democratic Convention" (July 29, 2004). Transcript available at <www.usatoday.com/news/politicselections/nation/president/2004-07-29-reagan-speech-text_x.htm>.

[22]Ibid.

[23]Ibid.

since they lack certain characteristics: they "have no fingers and toes, no brain or spinal cord. They have no thoughts, no fears. They feel no pain."[24] And because the cells that make up the tiny bodies of these early embryos have yet to develop into the cells of particular organs or systems (i.e., they have not differentiated), an early embryo conceived in a laboratory, so that researchers may use its stem cells, is merely "undifferentiated cells multiplying in a tissue culture" and not "a living, breathing person—parent, a spouse, a child."[25]

Ironically, by classifying early embryos as morally outside the circle of legal protection, Ron Reagan enters the arena of theological exploration on a question of philosophical anthropology. (Philosophical anthropology deals with questions about the nature of human beings, such as what constitutes a human being, whether human beings have immaterial natures, souls or minds, and/or whether the absence or presence of those attributes or properties determines a human being's status as a moral subject.) The younger Reagan chooses to answer a question of scholarly interest to theologians and philosophers (What is man?) in order to justify a particular act (the killing of embryos). He refers to the position of his adversaries as "an article of faith," even though he chooses to answer precisely the same question (What is man?) his adversaries answer. His adversaries' answer justifies forbidding the same act Reagan seeks to permit, killing early embryos. As anyone familiar with the literature on this subject will tell you, those who defend the position that the unborn are persons from conception offer reasons that are parts of arguments with conclusions.[26] These conclusions indeed may be, for many of their advocates, articles of faith, but they are also, in the considered judgments of these thoughtful citi-

---

[24]Ibid.

[25]Ibid.

[26]See, for example, Patrick Lee, *Abortion and Unborn Human Life* (Washington, D.C.: Catholic University of America Press, 1996); Patrick Lee, "The Prolife Argument from Substantial Identity: A Defense," *Bioethics* 18, no. 3 (2004): 249-63; Robert P. George and Alfonso Gòmez Lobo, "Personal Statement," in *Human Cloning and Human Dignity: An Ethical Inquiry,* by The President's Council on Bioethics (Washington, D.C.: President's Council on Bioethics, 2002): 258-66; J. P. Moreland and Scott B. Rae, *Body and Soul: Human Nature and the Crisis in Ethics* (Downers Grove, Ill.: InterVarsity Press, 2000); Francis J. Beckwith, *Defending Life: A Moral and Legal Case Against Abortion Choice* (New York: Cambridge University Press, 2007).

zens, deliverances of reason as well. Surely, these citizens may be mistaken about the strength of their arguments, but they are in no worse a position than Ron Reagan and those who offer different reasons for a contrary position, since they too may be mistaken about the strength of their arguments. In my opinion, because the younger Reagan and his allies do not consider beliefs informed by theology as belonging to a knowledge tradition, they feel justified in dismissing theologically informed policy proposals as de facto inferior to so-called secular ones, even when secular ones answer precisely the same questions as the so-called articles of faith. The younger Reagan and his allies offer no reasons for this apartheid of knowledge, since they know that convincing their peers that a view is or may be "religious" relieves them of their duty to rationally assess that view as a serious contender to the deliverances of so-called secular reason.[27]

St. Peter and the apostles, of course, explicitly defended their knowledge of Christ's lordship to a religious body that believed the apostles' claim to be false. Fortunately, many Western Christians live in nations in which their religious liberty does not depend on whether they can make a case for the veracity of their faith. This is because, ironically, as many scholars have argued,[28] the very idea of religious liberty springs from a Christian view of human beings that entails religious liberty as

---

[27]Ironically, Reagan's father, in a 1983 article, answered his son's argument over two decades before the younger Reagan uttered it:

> Regrettably, we live at a time when some persons do not value all human life. They want to pick and choose which individuals have value. Some have said that only those individuals with "consciousness of self" are human beings. One such writer has followed this deadly logic and concluded that "shocking as it may seem, a newly born infant is not a human being."
>
> A Nobel Prize winning scientist has suggested that if a handicapped child "were not declared fully human until three days after birth, then all parents could be allowed the choice." In other words, "quality control" to see if newly born human beings are up to snuff.
>
> Obviously, some influential people want to deny that every human life has intrinsic, sacred worth. They insist that a member of the human race must have certain qualities before they accord him or her status as a "human being." (Ronald W. Reagan, "Abortion and the Conscience of the Nation," *Human Life Review* [Spring 1983], National Review Online <www.nationalreview.com/document/reagan200406101030.asp>)

[28]See, for example, Michael Novak, "Is Religious Liberty for Everyone?" Third Annual Margaret Thatcher Freedom Lecture (May 29, 2007), The Heritage Foundation <www.aei.org /publications/pubID.26262/pub_detail.asp>.

a fundamental right that all persons possess. Denominations as different as the Southern Baptist Convention[29] and the Roman Catholic Church[30] embrace this understanding and defend it as a natural outgrowth of Christian principles found in both Scripture and church history. Sadly, Christians have at times failed to see this insight and to apply it justly to non-Christians under their political authority. For this reason, Christians should enter the public square with an understanding and sensitivity to the concerns of some of our fellow citizens who view certain policy proposals as an attempt to "force Christian religious views on others." This, of course, is a caricature, as our assessment of Ron Reagan's argument clearly shows. But these fellow citizens can hardly be blamed for their reaction, given the less-than-fair, and sometimes hysterically conspiratorial,[31] portrayal of conservative Christians in the popular media, as well as the sometimes misleading presentation of the virtues and vices of our Christian predecessors in the history of Western civilization.[32]

The same St. Peter who courageously stood up for the gospel in the book of Acts says in his first epistle that in this world those who follow Jesus are "aliens and exiles," and that they ought to "conduct [themselves] honorably among the Gentiles [i.e., unbelievers], so that, though they malign [them] as evildoers, they may see [their] honorable deeds and glorify God when he comes to judge" (1 Pet 2:11-12 NRSV). St. Peter goes on to write:

For the Lord's sake accept the authority of every human institution,

---

[29]See "Religious Liberty," The Ethics & Religious Liberty Commission of the Southern Baptist Convention website (2009) <http://erlc.com/topics/C33/>.

[30]See *Dignitas Humanae* (December 7, 1965), The Vatican <www.vatican.va/archive/hist_councils/ii_vatican_council/documents/vat-ii_decl_19651207_dignitatis-humanae_en.html>.

[31]See, for example, Barbara Forrest and Paul R. Gross, *Creationism's Trojan Horse: The Wedge of Intelligent Design*, rev. ed. (New York: Oxford University Press, 2007); Michelle Goldberg, *Kingdom Coming: The Rise of Christian Nationalism* (New York: W. W. Norton, 2006); Chris Hedges, *American Fascists: The Christian Right and the War on America* (New York: Free Press, 2007); and Kevin Phillips, *American Theocracy: The Peril and Politics of Radical Religion, Oil, and Borrowed Money in the 21st Century* (New York: Viking Adult, 2006).

[32]There are numerous correctives to this misleading history, two of which I highly recommend: Rodney Stark, *For the Glory of God: How Monotheism Led to Reformations, Science, Witch-Hunts, and the End of Slavery* (Princeton, N.J.: Princeton University Press, 2003); and Thomas E. Woods Jr., *How the Catholic Church Built Western Civilization* (Chicago: Regnery, 2005).

whether of the emperor as supreme, or of governors, as sent by him to punish those who do wrong and to praise those who do right. For it is God's will that by doing right you should silence the ignorance of the foolish. As servants of God, live as free people, yet do not use your freedom as a pretext for evil. Honor everyone. Love the family of believers. Fear God. Honor the emperor. (1 Pet 2:13-17 NRSV)

So, the Christian must use his freedom wisely and be honorable to his unbelieving neighbors as well as accept and respect the rule of law and the authorities put in place to protect it, all for the sake of the common good. In a liberal democracy, such as the United States, as noted previously, the Christian citizen has unprecedented access to the levers of power in comparison to her predecessors in the ancient and medieval worlds. For this reason, St. Peter's instructions, as well as the examples of St. Peter and St. Paul in the book of Acts, may have more practical application today than at any time in the 1,500 years following the establishment of the first century church.

SUPPORTING NON-CHRISTIAN CANDIDATES

Although no one is quite sure whether he actually uttered it, many claim the Protestant reformer Martin Luther said that he would rather be ruled by a competent Turk than an incompetent Christian. To many Christians, this precept makes sense. But other Christians would rather be governed by Christians than non-Christians. I'm with Martin Luther on this one, and I think that most Christians are as well once they take the time to think about it.

There are a wide variety of non-Christian citizens who reside in liberal democracies such as the United States. We are familiar with many of them, both from history and in contemporary times. The third president of the United States, Thomas Jefferson (1743-1826), was a deist and not a Christian. Deists believe in God, insofar as they believe that a personal God created the universe with scientific and moral laws that can be detected and known by human reason. But they do not believe that God intervenes with nature. Christians, on the other hand, believe that God has acted in history and (in particular) in the person of Jesus Christ, the second person of the triune God. Although few people these days identify themselves as deists, there are many non-Christians who serve and have served in the U.S. government, including Jews, Christian Scientists, Unitarians and Mormons. In 2000, Senator Joseph Lieberman of Connecticut, an Orthodox Jew, was the vice presidential running mate of the Democratic Party's presidential candidate, then–Vice President Al Gore. Former governor of Massachusetts Mitt Romney, a Mormon, ran competitively for the 2008 Republican presidential nomination, which was eventually won by Senator John McCain of Arizona. In 2006, Rep. Keith Ellison (D-MN) became the first Muslim elected to the U.S. Congress.

Given what we have covered in this chapter concerning a Christian's responsibilities as a citizen, this section moves on toward providing Christians with a way to think through the question of voting for a non-Christian. To accomplish this, I will focus on one religious tradition, Mormonism, though I could have selected any number of other faiths such as Islam, Judaism or Hinduism.

As has been aptly documented,[33] the foundational beliefs of the Church of Jesus Christ of Latter-day Saints (i.e., the LDS church or the Mormon Church) are contrary to those held by the three branches of Christendom: Catholic, Protestant and Orthodox. These unique Mormon beliefs include belief in a corporeal, finite God who is an exalted and perfect man, an uncreated universe for which God is not the first cause, a doctrine of salvation (or exaltation) that promises divine status to its recipients, and extrabiblical scriptures and prophetic revelation contrary to the catholic creeds of Christendom.

Founded in 1830 in upstate New York, the Mormon church's central message was that authentic Christianity had lost the true gospel only a few generations after Jesus' original disciples had died. (Mormons are unclear on precisely when this total apostasy was complete, but it surely had to have occurred prior to the formulation of the A.D. 325 Nicene Creed, which the LDS church rejects.) True Christianity, Mormons say, had vanished from the earth for roughly 1,500 to 1,700 years, until a fourteen-year-old resident of Palmyra, New York, named Joseph

---

[33]See, for example, Francis J. Beckwith, Carol Mosser and Paul Owen, eds., *The New Mormon Challenge* (Grand Rapids: Zondervan, 2002).

Smith Jr., as he claimed, received an answer to his prayer and was personally visited by God the Father and his Son, Jesus Christ. Smith was instructed by them to join none of the Christian churches. This is when Mormons believe Smith began his cooperation with God and his Son in the restoration of the true gospel.

Part of the restoration included a new set of inspired scriptures, the first of which was the Book of Mormon (1830), which contains the story of the resurrected Christ visiting America and preaching and teaching his gospel to its native peoples. According to the LDS narrative, Smith translated the Book of Mormon from gold plates that were buried in New York's Hill Cumorah, a location that was revealed to him by the Angel Moroni. Another aspect of the restoration included a new ecclesiastical structure based on apostolic succession and the passing on of priestly authority without requiring a special class of clerics. According to Smith, in 1829 John the Baptist visited Smith and his friend Oliver Cowdery and bestowed on them the Aaronic priesthood, which empowered its recipients to preach, baptize, ordain others and perform Levitical duties. Smith claimed that soon after receiving the Aaronic priesthood, he and Cowdery were visited by the apostles Peter, James and John, who literally laid hands on Smith and Cowdery in order to restore the Melchizedek priesthood. This bestowed on them apostolic status as well as the power to administer ordinances, promulgate doctrine, and organize and lead the church. The Mormon Church, which began in 1830 with only a handful of American followers, has mushroomed to nearly thirteen million members worldwide.

Now suppose that one of the major U.S. political parties nominates a Mormon to be its candidate for the U.S. presidency. This is not difficult to do since, in 2008, Governor Romney was such a candidate, though he lost in the primaries. Christian citizens must exercise great caution in this type of situation. They must not ignore their commitment to justice and the common good when assessing such a candidate. One mistake is to be inordinately concerned with a candidate's creedal allegiance to a particular faith, which may cloud people's judgment and cause them to ignore or play down the point of politics—to do justice and advance the common good. But the candidate has to be careful as well. He or she

should realize that traditional Christians will be watching very carefully
to see if the candidate will make the mistake of trivializing or sequestering his or her own faith, which would offend many traditional Christians who would have offered their support. The latter I call the Kennedy mistake, and the former, the confessional mistake.

The Kennedy mistake. In 1960, Senator John F. Kennedy, a Roman
Catholic, was the Democratic Party's candidate for the U.S. presidency.
He was to become the first Catholic president in a country whose citizenry had been predominantly Protestant, and pugnaciously anti-
Catholic, since its infancy. Many Protestant Christians were concerned
that Kennedy's commitment as a Catholic Christian to the teaching of
the church's Magisterium on a variety of social, moral and political issues would serve as his guide for U.S. domestic and foreign policy. In
order to assuage Protestant fears, on September 12, 1960, Senator Kennedy addressed the Greater Houston Ministerial Association and as-
sured the attendees that nothing of his Catholic faith would play any
role in his judgments as occupant of the White House:

> I am not the Catholic candidate for President. I am the Democratic
> Party's candidate for President who happens also to be a Catholic. I do
> not speak for my church on public matters—and the church does not
> speak for me.
>
> Whatever issue may come before me as President—on birth control,
> divorce, censorship, gambling or any other subject—I will make my de-
> cision in accordance with these views [i.e., religious liberty and church-
> state separation], in accordance with what my conscience tells me to be
> the national interest, and without regard to outside religious pressures
> or dictates. And no power or threat of punishment could cause me to
> decide otherwise.[34]

From the vantage point of the early twenty-first century, Senator
Kennedy's speech reads like a complete acquiescence to American
mainline Protestant notions of privatized faith and anticlericalism as
well as its stereotypical, outdated and uncharitable ideas about the
Catholic hierarchy and the teachings of the Catholic Church. Senator

---

[34]John F. Kennedy, "Address to the Greater Houston Ministerial Association" (September 12,
1960), QuoteDB <www.quotedb.com/speeches/greater-houston-ministerial-association>.

Kennedy could have argued that his Catholicism informed him of certain theological and moral doctrines that would make him a thoughtful and principled president. He could have consulted and mined from the works of Catholic scholars such as Jacques Maritain or John Courtney Murray, both of whom were able defenders of liberal democracy and the natural law that grounds it. In fact, Senator Kennedy's speechwriter, Ted Sorenson, according to an article in *The Catholic World Report*, "said that he had vetted the Houston speech with . . . Murray, . . . chief architect of the Second Vatican Council's landmark affirmation of religious freedom. But most historians agree that Murray disapproved of the strident separationism that Kennedy championed."[35] Senator Kennedy's speech was a terrible concession. It played to his audience's anti-Catholic prejudices while saying that his religious beliefs were so trivial that he would govern exactly the same if they were absent.

A Mormon presidential candidate, in order to pacify traditional Christians (including evangelicals and Catholics), may be tempted to emulate Senator Kennedy and claim that his theology and church do not influence or shape his politics. There are at least two reasons why this would be a mistake.

First, such a move would signal to traditional Christians that the candidate does not believe that theology could in principle count as knowledge. But this is precisely the view of the secularist who believes that religion, like matters of taste, should remain entirely private. But if a citizen has good reason to believe his theological tradition offers real insights into the nature of humanity and the common good—insights that could be defended on grounds that even a secularist may find persuasive—why should he remain mute simply because the secularist stipulates a definition of religion that requires his silence? Why should she accept the secularist's limitations on her religious liberty based on what appears to many of us as a capricious and politically convenient understanding of "religion"? If a Mormon candidate were to commit the Kennedy mistake, he or she would give tacit permission to secular-

---

[35]Colleen Carroll Campbell, "The Enduring Costs of John F. Kennedy's Compromise," *The Catholic World Report* (February 2007), Colleen Carroll Campbell website <www.colleen -campbell.com/articles/020107JFK.htm>.

ists to call into question the political legitimacy of potential natural allies, conservative Catholics and evangelicals.

Second, it is not the case that non-Christian traditions lack resources with which traditional Christians could agree and which could give them confidence in the candidate. For example, even though I believe that LDS theology is fundamentally non-Christian, this does not mean that it does not include beliefs that many secularists and traditional Christians would find defensible or even consistent with their own views. If that is in fact the case, as I believe it is, then an LDS candidate may be able to argue that because of his theological beliefs, rather than in spite of them, he is deeply committed to certain principles of justice and liberal democracy that require that the government protect certain inalienable rights like those mentioned in the Declaration of Independence and the U.S. Constitution's Bill of Rights. To cite but one example, in the Doctrine & Covenants (132: 1, 3, 5) part of the LDS canon of scripture, the Mormon prophet Joseph Smith Jr., states:

> We believe that governments were instituted of God for the benefit of man. . . . We believe that all governments necessarily require civil officers and magistrates to enforce the laws of the same; and that such as will administer the law in equity and justice should be sought for and upheld by the voice of the people if a republic, or the will of the sovereign. . . . We believe that all men are bound to sustain and uphold their respective governments in which they reside, while protected in their inherent and inalienable rights by the laws of such governments . . . and that all governments have a right to enact such laws as their own judgments have best calculated to secure the public interest.

My point is that non-Christian candidates may have at their disposal theological resources that, though not shared by Christians, may help Christians and other non-Christian citizens see that the principles of liberal democracy are integral to the candidate's worldview and understanding of a just society. This, of course, does not require the Christian to accept that this candidate's religious beliefs are "just as true" as his own. That is not the issue. The issue is whether the candidate's beliefs—true or not—play an integral role in shaping the candidate's political philosophy.

The confessional mistake. This mistake occurs when a Christian citizen believes that the planks of his creed or theological confession—for example, the Nicene Creed, the Westminster Confession—are the best standard by which to judge the suitability of a candidate running for public office. For example, suppose a Presbyterian elder votes for candidate X solely on the basis that her opponent, candidate Y, rejects the Nicene Creed and the Westminster Confession. An elder who did this would not truly understand the purpose of creeds and confessions. For their purpose is to provide to church members and the world at large a summary of beliefs that one must embrace in order to be considered an orthodox member of that body. Creeds and confessions are not meant to measure the qualifications of a political candidate in a liberal democracy. Not only do Christendom's most important creeds and confessions predate the existence of liberal democracies, their subject matter bears no relation to assessing those attributes that we consider essential to the leadership of a political regime. In practice, most Christians already fully grasp this truth.

For example, many evangelicals in the 1980 presidential election voted for Ronald W. Reagan over Jimmy Carter, even though President Carter was perceived at the time to be more evangelical in his theology and church participation than then-Governor Reagan. For Reagan's supporters, his policies and not his theology were decisive for them. Although at the time these evangelicals would have likely chosen Carter over Reagan to teach Sunday school, they preferred Reagan in the Oval Office because they believed that Reagan's policies best advanced the common good.

Is there scriptural warrant for the notion that the common good should be the standard by which we assess candidates? Although I believe the answer is yes, as I have argued above, one must exercise care in using Scripture to address this sort of question. For, as I have already noted, the Bible's authors did not reside in liberal democracies in which citizens play an integral part in electing their leaders, shaping policy and enforcing laws. So, this is how I suggest one should proceed: if we assume that the common good is achieved when a political regime treats justly its citizens and the many institutions that help develop and sustain their virtue (e.g., families, schools, churches, etc.), it seems that the Bible does provide us principles by which we can evaluate those running for public office.

To illustrate what I mean, I will briefly review some of the principles we covered above that seem to show how the Scriptures instruct the state and the individual to do justice in a variety of different ways.

The stranger is my neighbor. Jesus tells us to love our neighbors as ourselves (Lk 10:27) and offers the parable of the Good Samaritan in order to illustrate that the stranger too is my neighbor and entitled to be treated justly (Lk 10:29-37).

Help the less fortunate. We are commanded to help the poor, feed the hungry, clothe the naked and comfort the afflicted (Mt 25:31-46; Jas 1:26-27). This can be accomplished by churches or by government programs. (Some Christians, as I noted above, like Marvin Olasky, emphasize the former, while others, like Jim Wallis, stress the latter.)

The state should be just. The Old Testament is replete with calls for justice and condemnations of injustice directed to the state (e.g., Deut 24:19-22; Prov 31:8-9; Is 58:6-10).

There is a rightly-ordered social fabric. The Ten Commandments (Ex 20:2-17) tell us something of God's plan for a rightly ordered society. We are to worship God, honor our mothers and fathers, remain faithful to our spouses, not covet or steal our neighbors' property or spouse, maintain integrity in word and deed, and respect the intrinsic dignity of human life. In present-day political terms this can translate to the government respecting and privileging religious liberty, the right to life, private property, traditional marriage, male-female parenthood and integrity in public life.

It should be noted that many Christian scholars defend these principles as not only biblical but also as the deliverances of natural reason apart from Scripture.[36] This is why there are many non-Christians who

---

[36]See, for example, C. S. Lewis, *The Abolition of Man* (London: Oxford University Press, 1943); Norman L. Geisler, *Thomas Aquinas: An Evangelical Assessment* (Grand Rapids: Baker, 1991), pp. 163-75; J. Daryl Charles, "Protestants and Natural Law," *First Things* 168 (December 2006): 33-38; Michael Bauman, *Pilgrim Theology: Taking the Path of Theological Discovery* (Grand Rapids: Zondervan, 1992), pp. 203-8; Francis J. Beckwith and Gregory P. Koukl, *Relativism: Feet Firmly Planted in Mid-Air* (Grand Rapids: Baker, 1998); David VanDrunen, *A*

agree with Christians on these principles, even if these non-Christians reject some if not all of the Christian Bible as God's Word. After all, as I have noted in several places in this chapter, many of the calls for justice in Scripture, such as in the case of Cain's murder of Abel, presuppose that the reader already knows what constitutes justice apart from any special revelation from God.

Nevertheless, a candidate who embraces these ideals, even if he or she is not a Christian, is a candidate that a Christian can support with a clear conscience. So, can a Christian vote for a non-Christian? Absolutely. In fact, in some cases a Christian's conscience may require he support a non-Christian candidate if that candidate is the best-situated person who is most likely to advance the common good.

Conclusion

It seems clear that because Christians in a liberal democracy have the historically unique power to enact laws that advance the common good, they have a special obligation to take their citizenship seriously and use good judgment in voting and supporting legislation and political candidates. This is not to say that Christians will always agree on the proper route by which the government ought to advance the common good. But there is no doubt that they have a biblical mandate to advance it.

Biblical Case for Natural Law (Grand Rapids: The Acton Institute, 2006); Alan F. Johnson, "Is There Biblical Warrant for Natural Law Theory?" *Journal of the Evangelical Theological Society* 25, no. 2 (June 1982): 185-99.

3

The Separation
of Church and State

Although virtually all American citizens claim to believe in the separation of church and state, difficulties arise when they start discussing specific issues. For example, some who hold to church-state separation believe that the government should not provide tax-supported vouchers to parents who want to use those vouchers to help pay for their children's education at private religious schools. Other citizens, equally adamant in their support of church-state separation, hold that if the government excludes religious schools from such a voucher program it would be singling out religious education for special punishment that is not meted out to private secular schools.

In this chapter we will first take a brief historical survey of the meaning of church-state separation and how it has morphed from an idea that rejected the union of the institutions of church and state to the view that religious ideas held by serious religious believers should not be reflected in public policy. We will then examine how the meaning of religious free exercise has been altered in a way that seems hostile to religious belief.

RELIGION AND THE U.S. CONSTITUTION
The United States Constitution addresses religion in only two places. The first is in article VI, in which a religious test for a federal office in the United States is prohibited.[1] The other place is in the First Amend-

---

[1]See Francis J. Beckwith, "The Court of Disbelief: The Constitution's Article VI Religious Test Prohibition and the Judiciary's Religious Motive Analysis," *Hastings Constitutional Law Quarterly* 33, nos. 2/3 (Winter and Spring 2006): 337-60.

ment of the Bill of Rights, which contains a sequence of words that many Americans can recite by memory: "Congress shall make no law respecting an establishment of religion, or prohibiting the free exercise thereof . . ."[2]

This portion of the First Amendment is often said to have two "clauses," an establishment clause (the first part) and a free-exercise clause (the second part). The establishment clause is sometimes called a "disestablishment clause," since it is stating that Congress may not employ its legislative power to establish an official national religion. The free-exercise clause is sometimes called the "religious liberty clause," since it is asserting that the Constitution protects the religious liberty of citizens from any legislative act of Congress.

The phrase "separation of church and state" has been employed by many as a shorthand way to describe the legal principles that they believe are the basis for the religion clauses of the First Amendment. But the religion clauses are notoriously vague, for they give us no direction as to the precise meaning of "free exercise," "establishment" or even "religion."

The text clearly indicates, however, that the First Amendment was intended to limit the law-making power of Congress and not any other branch of the state or federal governments. But since the early twentieth century, the Supreme Court began applying (in a piecemeal fashion) the First Amendment to all governments in the United States.[3] It was not until 1947, in the case of *Everson v. Board of Education*,[4] that the Supreme Court would apply the establishment clause to a nonfederal government. It justified this move by a doctrine of constitutional interpretation known as incorporation: the fundamental rights of citizens protected by the Fourteenth Amendment (adopted in 1868; in short, that life, liberty and property may not be abridged without legal due process) imply most of the rights in the Bill of Rights, including the

---

[2]U.S. Constitution, amend. 1.

[3]The Court first incorporated the freedom of speech and press clauses, eventually incorporating the entire First Amendment. See *Gitlow v. New York*, 268 U.S. 652, 666 (1925); *Near v. Minnesota*, 283 U.S. 697, 707 (1931); *De Jorge v. Oregon*, 299 U.S. 353, 364 (1937); *Cantwell v. Connecticut*, 310 U.S. 296, 303-304 (1940); and *Everson v. Board of Education*, 330 U.S. 1 (1947).

[4]*Everson v. Board of Education*, 330 U.S. 1 (1947).

rights that are found in the First Amendment.[5] That is, these First Amendment rights (including both religion clauses) are incorporated through the Fourteenth Amendment. Whether such a move is justified is outside the scope of this chapter. Needless to say, even if it is not justified, Americans have grown so accustomed to thinking of their federal constitutional rights as restraints on all governments—federal, state and local—that even a logically sound argument against incorporation is not likely to get very far.

The notion of "separation of church and state" exists as a largely unquestioned dogma in American political and legal discourse, even though the phrase does not appear in the text of the Constitution and a plain reading of the religion clauses is just as consistent with some forms of moderate separationism as it is with strong separationism.

Although it is difficult to define precisely the differences between moderate separationism and strong separationism, it seems to me that the following is a fair distinction: (1) Both affirm that the government should maximize religious liberty consistent with the public good, as well as prohibit both ecclesiastical control of government powers and government control of ecclesiastical powers. (2) Moderate separationism does not attempt to exclude religion from public life, and thus would, for example, support public funding for programs of similarly situated religious and secular entities.

On the other hand, strong separationism forbids any direct aid to religion even when similarly situated secular entities are given aid. In addition, strong separationists seem willing to exclude the political proposals of religious citizens if those proposals are religiously motivated, though similarly situated nonreligious citizens who offer proposals based on secular grounds are unlikely to suffer the same fate.[6]

---

[5]There are disagreements among jurists as to what aspects or provisions of the Bill of Rights should be incorporated through the Fourteenth Amendment. For a brief summary of these different views, see Doug Linder, "The Incorporation Debate," Exploring Constitutional Conflicts page (May 25, 2004) <www.law.umkc.edu/faculty/projects/ftrials/conlaw/incorp.htm>.
[6]See Thomas C. Berg, "Anti-Catholicism and Modern Church-State Relations," *Loyola University of Chicago Law Journal* (Fall 2001): 122 n. 5. See also Douglas Laycock, "The Underlying Unity of Separation and Neutrality," *Emory Law Journal* 46 (1997): 43-74; and Carl H. Esbeck, "Myths, Miscues, and Misconceptions: No-Aid Separationism and the Establishment Clause," *Notre Dame Journal of Law, Ethics & Public Policy* 13 (1999): 285-319.

So, a school voucher program that included all schools—public, private secular and private religious—is consistent with moderate separationism because the state is not showing preference or disdain for a specific religious group. On the other hand, for a strong separationist, a voucher program that excludes religious schools is good, for when the government underwrites a religious program it places the state in the position of supporting the church. And for many strong separationists a church or church-sponsored school that receives government funding puts the government in a position of leverage over the church. This, some argue, may compromise the integrity of the church's mission to preach the gospel and be a prophetic voice in the wider culture.

Story of a Slogan

In his masterful work *Separation of Church and State*,[7] Philip Hamburger shows why separationism has achieved its dominant status in American politics and jurisprudence. He argues that it is the result of an ambiguous slogan—*separation of church and state*—that was first seriously employed in American politics during the mid- to late-nineteenth century to advance a particular view of religion, state and liberty, a view that proponents claim is the "American way." This is not to say that the "separation of church and state" is not a good thing or not consistent with the American understanding of liberal democracy. There is no doubt that it is. But, as we have already seen in our brief look at moderate and strong separationism, devout citizens of good will are going to disagree on precisely what separationism means. Hamburger tells the story of this slogan, which was famously employed by President Thomas Jefferson (1743-1826) in his 1802 letter to the Danbury Baptists:

> Believing with you that religion is a matter which lies solely between man and his God, that he owes account to none other for his faith or his worship, that the legislative powers of government reach actions only, and not opinions, I contemplate the sovereign reverence that act of the whole American people which declared that their legislature should "make no law respecting an establishment of religion, or prohibiting the

---

[7]Philip Hamburger, *Separation of Church and State* (Cambridge, Mass.: Harvard University Press, 2002).

free exercise thereof," thus building a wall of separation between Church & State.[8]

Because Jefferson is one of America's Founding Fathers, this letter—which Jefferson wrote as president—has the status of a sacred text in both strong and moderate separationist circles. Among some strong separationists, Jefferson's letter to the Danbury Baptists carries with it an authority not unlike Paul's letter to the Galatians. And yet, Jefferson's letter is, after all, a type of communication that presidents produce at least several times a day to a wide range of constituencies. Given that, it seems somewhat dubious to base constitutional doctrine on what amounts to nothing more than a note to political allies seeking the president's support for their religious liberty. This note was not part of an executive order, proposed legislation or even a directive offered by the president to the attorney general as a suggested way to interpret the establishment clause. It is not clear, therefore, why one should take Jefferson's letter to the Baptists as any more normative for constitutional interpretation as, let's say, Ronald Reagan's published book defending the prolife position on abortion,[9] since after all, Reagan as California governor signed into law one of the first statutes that significantly liberalized access to abortion.[10] Because the California law predated *Roe v. Wade* (1973) by six years, Governor Reagan was one of legalized abortion's "founding fathers" and thus perhaps possessed a special insight into the issue's jurisprudence.

Hamburger points out that Jefferson's letter embodied a particular understanding of the relationship between church and state that was not even shared by the recipients of the letter, the Danbury Baptists, who were known as dissenters, those who opposed religious establishment but did not oppose the influence of religion on government.[11] In a sense, then, the Danbury Baptists were moderate separationists while

---

[8]Thomas Jefferson, *Letter to the Danbury Baptists* (January 1, 1802), Library of Congress <www.loc.gov/loc/lcib/9806/danpre.html>.

[9]Ronald W. Reagan, *Abortion and the Conscience of the Nation* (Nashville: Thomas Nelson, 1984).

[10]See Carole Joffe, "30 Years After *Roe v. Wade:* Lessons about Abortion from the San Francisco Nine," Pro-Choice Forum (January 2003) <www.prochoiceforum.org.uk/ocrabortlaw6.asp>.

[11]Hamburger, *Separation*, pp. 163-80.

Jefferson was a strong separationist (if we were to use contemporary labels). According to Hamburger, "Jefferson's letter was not entirely a declaration of liberty. Separation was an idea first introduced into American politics by Jefferson's allies, the Republicans, who used it to elicit popular distaste against Federalist clergymen in their exercise of their religious freedom."[12] (The Federalists and the Democratic-Republicans [referred to in the quote above as "Republicans"] were the two major political parties in early America.) For the Federalist clergy had "inveighed against Jefferson, often from their pulpits, excoriating his infidelity and deism."[13] (Deism, as I noted in chapter 2, is the view held by some of America's Founding Fathers that God created the world with a discoverable scientific and moral order, but that God did not miraculously interfere with his creation. Hence, Jefferson, though a believer in a personal God, was not a Christian, since Christianity requires one to believe that God acted miraculously in history, such as in the resurrection of Christ.) Although "[t]he religious dissenters, including the Baptists, sympathized with the Republicans and distrusted the Federalists, particularly the Federalist clergy[,] . . . when invited by Jefferson to join the Republican demand for separation, the Baptists quietly declined."[14]

Because it was assumed that the moral ecology of a society could not be maintained without the influence of religion, dissenters constantly had to deal with the false charge that they were really separationists who wanted to remove any vestiges of religion from the public square. This is why, as Hamburger points out, "the Baptists who sought the support of the president were silent about his letter."[15] For Jefferson's letter would have been counterproductive in quelling the fears of those who equated antiestablishment with separationism. As Hamburger notes, "[I]t may be useful to begin by considering the [Baptists'] awkward situation. . . . [E]stablishment ministers had long accused dissenters of advocating separation, whether of church from state or religion

---

[12]Ibid., pp. 109-10.
[13]Ibid., p. 111.
[14]Ibid., p. 110.
[15]Ibid., p. 165.

from government." But "Baptists merely sought disestablishment and did not challenge the widespread assumption that republican government depended upon the people's morals and thus upon religion."[16]

The Danbury Baptists, like most Americans at the time, maintained that the church and state were two separate spheres, but that the church, like other nongovernment institutions, played a vital role in civilizing the nation's citizens and instilling in them the notion that their rights were not derived from the fiat of governments but rather were stamped on them by their Creator. The role of government is to protect the people's God-given rights while the role of religion is to shape the moral understanding of the nation's people so that they may be upright citizens.

According to this view, the United States of America is a constitutional republic whose institutions presuppose and entail certain beliefs about the order and nature of conditions necessary for maintaining the continuity and purpose of the nation, including the rights of its people and the powers of its governments (both state and federal). The philosophical infrastructure of the American republic consists of a cluster of ideals, beliefs, practices and institutions that are best sustained by a people who see this cluster as grounded in certain unchanging moral truths that are religious in nature. As I argue elsewhere in this book (chapter 5), liberal democracy assumes certain moral truths about human beings that are best grounded in God.

Given this understanding, the Danbury Baptists were troubled that their state, Connecticut, levied a tax to support the state's established religion, Congregationalism. Connecticut did allow Baptists and other citizens to request that the state redirect their tax money to their own churches, but the process required that "they first had to obtain, fill out, and properly file an exemption certificate." And because "Baptists were a harassed minority, some communities made it difficult for them to receive these exemptions."[17] This is why they shared their complaint with President Jefferson. But they, like many Americans at the time,[18]

---

[16]Ibid.

[17]Derek H. Davis, "Thomas Jefferson and the 'Wall of Separation' Metaphor," *Journal of Church and State* 45, no. 1 (Winter 2003): 10.

[18]Of course, establishment supporters did see antiestablishment dissenters as no different than separationists. See Hamburger, *Separation*, pp. 65-78.

did not see their resistance to religious establishment as inconsistent with a government that accommodates and sometimes encourages its people to embrace an account of rights and human institutions in which religion and its moral instruction are essential.

ANTI-CATHOLIC PREJUDICE AND THE TRIUMPH OF SEPARATIONISM

In the nineteenth century a form of strong separationism surged to prominence, largely as a Protestant reaction against the influx of immigrants from predominantly Roman Catholic countries. Some of these immigrant groups, which included the Irish and Italians, set up their own private religious schools. Many non-Catholic Americans believed well into the twentieth century that Catholic schools indoctrinated their students with superstitions that were inconsistent with the principles of American democracy. Take, for example, these comments by the influential Baptist church-state separationist, the Reverend Joseph Martin Dawson:

> The Catholics, who are now [in 1948] claiming a near majority over all Protestants in the United States, would abolish our public school system which is our greatest single factor in national unity and would substitute their old-world, medieval parochial schools, with their alien culture. Or else they make it plain that they wish to install facilities for teaching their religion in the public schools. . . . Perhaps the burning issue has arisen soon enough to enable the friends of the native American culture to arrest the progress of the long-range plan of those who would supplant it. There can be no doubt about the Catholic plan. Having lost enormous prestige in Europe, the church now looks to the United States as a suitable stage for the recovery of its lost influence. Here it would seek new ground, consolidate and expand, as compensation for its weakened position in bankrupt Europe, with the hope of transforming this continent, a Protestant country, into a Catholic citadel from which to exert a powerful rule. If this seems exaggerated and fanciful, the reader has only to open his eyes to what the Catholics are doing to achieve this end.[19]

In order to make sure that such schools would not receive govern-

---

[19]J. M. Dawson, *Separate Church and State Now* (New York: R. R. Smith, 1948), p. 96.

ment funding of any sort, federal and state legislation was proposed that would forbid the use of public resources for "sectarian" (read: Catholic) religious purposes. The most ambitious attempt in the nineteenth century to put this understanding into law was a proposed constitutional amendment by Rep. James Blaine (R-ME):

> No State shall make any law respecting an establishment of religion or prohibiting the free exercise thereof; and no money raised by taxation in any State, for the support of public schools, or derived from any public fund therefore, nor any public lands devoted thereto, shall ever be under the control of any religious sect, nor shall any money so raised, or lands so devoted be divided between religious sects or denominations.[20]

Called the Blaine Amendment, it never became part of the Constitution. However, some individual states passed Blaine-type statutes or constitutional amendments that still remain on the books.[21]

Hamburger astutely points out that by arguing the need for these amendments, supporters of the Blaine Amendment and its progeny implicitly conceded that the First Amendment's establishment clause, by itself, did not prohibit the use of public resources for religious purposes. Of course, this would mean that separationist jurisprudence, which relies on a Blaine-type understanding of church and state for the federal Constitution, is likely not a proper reading of the First Amendment. This does not mean, of course, that some modest form of separationism, something like the traditional antiestablishment position of the Danbury Baptists, is not correct (as I believe is in fact the case). Rather, what it means is that a doctrine borne of anti-Catholic animus and a desire to declare an American Protestant hegemony as the established understanding of public faith is hardly the "neutral" and "separationist" creed its proponents have led us to believe. Ironically, as Hamburger points out, the underlying principles of separationism were picked up in the twentieth century by secularists hostile to all religion in public life

---

[20]4 *Congressional Record* 5453 (1876).

[21]For example, the Constitution of Texas states: "No money shall be appropriated, or drawn from the Treasury for the benefit of any sect, or religious society, theological or religious seminary; nor shall property belonging to the State be appropriated for any such purposes." Texas Constitution, art. 1, sec. 7, available at <www.capitol.state.tx.us/txconst/sections/cn000100 -000700.html>.

who then applied these principles to the cherished practices of many (though not all) nineteenth-century anti-Catholic Protestant separationists: teacher-led and school-sponsored prayer[22] and Bible reading in public schools.[23] These separationist principles were eventually applied critically by jurists and scholars to laws that reflected traditional moral understandings on abortion,[24] homosexuality,[25] physician-assisted suicide[26] and the nature of the embryo.[27] (Concerning the latter, in chapter 2, I briefly go over Ron Reagan's defense of federal funding of embryonic stem-cell research at the 2004 Democratic National Convention. In this present chapter, I will briefly discuss the question of abortion and its relationship to church-state separation.)

However, the most extreme application of this separationist point of view has to be the rejection by some scholars of the American Founders' notion that just government and constitutional jurisprudence presuppose human ability to know and apply unchanging moral truths.[28] Take, for example, the words of strong separationist law professor Steven G. Gey:

> The establishment clause should be viewed as a reflection of the secular, relativist political values of the Enlightenment, which are incompatible with the fundamental nature of religious faith. As an embodiment of these Enlightenment values, the establishment clause requires that the political influence of religion be substantially diminished. . . . Religious belief and practice should be protected under the first amendment, but only to the same extent and for the same reason that all other forms of expression and conscience are protected—because the first amendment

---

[22]See *Engel v. Vitale*, 370 U.S. 421 (1962) and *Wallace v. Jaffree*, 472 U.S. 38 (1985).

[23]*Abington School District v. Schenpp*, 374 U.S. 203 (1963).

[24]See *Webster v. Reproductive Health Services*, 492 U.S. 490, 566-67, 569 (1989), (Stevens, J., dissenting).

[25]See D. W. Machacek and A. Fulco, "The Courts and Public Discourse: The Case of Gay Marriage," *Journal of Church and State* 46, no. 4 (Autumn 2004): 767-85; *Bowers v. Hardwick*, 478 U.S. 186, 216 (1986), (Stevens, J., dissenting); *Lawrence v. Texas*, 539 U.S. 518, 525 (2003).

[26]See David McKenzie, "Church, State, and Physician-Assisted Suicide," *Journal of Church and State* 46, no. 4 (Autumn 2004): 787-809.

[27]See Paul D. Simmons, "Religious Liberty and Abortion Policy: *Casey* as 'Catch-22,'" *Journal of Church and State* 42, no. 1 (Winter 2000): 69-88.

[28]See Steven G. Gey, "Why Is Religion Special?: Reconsidering the Accommodation of Religion Under the Religion Clauses of the First Amendment," *University of Pittsburgh Law Review* 52 (Fall 1990): 75-187.

prohibits government from enacting into law any religious, political, or aesthetic orthodoxy. . . .

[R]eligious principles are not based on logic or reason, and, therefore, may not be proved or disproved. . . .

[R]eligion asserts that its principles are immutable and absolutely authoritative, democratic theory asserts just the opposite. The sine qua non of any democratic state is that everything political is open to question; not only specific policies and programs, but the very structure of the state itself must always be subject to challenge. Democracies are by nature inhospitable to political or intellectual stasis or certainty. Religion is fundamentally incompatible with this intellectual cornerstone of the modern democratic state. The irreconcilable distinction between democracy and religion is that, although there can be no sacrosanct principles or unquestioned truths in a democracy, no religion can exist without sacrosanct principles and unquestioned truths.[29]

One can raise several questions about Professor Gey's reasoning. First, his embracing of relativist political values (whatever those are) is self-refuting.[30] Relativism is the view that there are no universal and unchanging political values that apply to all persons in all times and all places. Yet Professor Gey states that a true proponent of liberal democracy ought to be a relativist, for he claims that liberal democracy and opposition to relativism are incompatible. But to claim that one ought to be a relativist is to make a nonrelative, normative claim about what it means for a member of the political community to be intellectually virtuous. Thus, Gey's claim refutes itself. On the other hand, if he denies that each member of a liberal democratic political community ought to be a relativist on the matter of political values, then necessarily it is not the case that each member of a liberal democratic political community ought to be a relativist on the matter of political values. Consequently, whether he affirms or denies his claim, Gey's claim is

---

[29]Ibid., pp. 79, 167, 174.

[30]For critiques of *moral* relativism and its application to political issues, see Francis J. Beckwith and Gregory P. Koukl, *Relativism: Feet Firmly Planted in Mid-Air* (Grand Rapids: Baker, 1998); Francis J. Beckwith, *Defending Life: A Moral and Legal Case Against Abortion Choice* (New York: Cambridge University Press, 2007), chap. 1; and Hadley Arkes, *First Things: An Inquiry into the First Principles of Morals and Justice* (Princeton, N.J.: Princeton University Press, 1986).

refuted, and thus we can safely say it is something that no friend of reason ought to entertain seriously.

Second, Gey associates his relativist view of liberal democracy with the Enlightenment, the period of intellectual history in Western Europe roughly between the late sixteenth and early nineteenth centuries, in which leading philosophers and thinkers argued that unaided human reason was the only basis for knowledge and thus for legitimate political, intellectual, moral and religious authority. But it is difficult to square Professor Gey's view of the Enlightenment with the nonrelativist moral and political philosophies of John Locke, Immanuel Kant and Adam Smith, whose Enlightenment credentials no one doubts.

Third, Gey claims that "there can be no sacrosanct principles or unquestioned truths in a democracy" and that "no religion can exist without sacrosanct principles and unquestioned truths."[31] But the latter claim is itself an unquestioned truth about which Gey seems certain. For he employs it as the ground by which the law may permanently sequester a large segment of fellow citizens from the public square simply because they may choose to shape their communities with policies that are informed by their religious beliefs. Moreover, Gey's position assumes a first principle—democracy ought not to be based on unquestioned truths—that he stipulates and for which he does not offer support, and thus seems to function as an unquestioned truth. But if Gey were to offer support for that truth, those grounds too would need support, and those grounds would then become the new first principle. At some point, therefore, Gey must rely on a first principle, a foundation, on which his claims about liberal democracy (and its support) may rationally rest and for which no other grounds are necessary. Thus, if, as Gey argues, the political application of "unquestioned truths" is a sufficient condition for the political disenfranchisement of fellow citizens, then his own position serves as the ground by which the state may disenfranchise him, since his philosophical arsenal has within it at least one unquestioned truth, namely, that "democracy ought not to be based on unquestioned truths." Consequently, Professor Gey's position is by

---

[31]Steven G. Gey, "Why Is Religion Special?" p. 174.

its own lights irrational, and thus we need not think of it as an impediment to the political participation of citizens who embrace what Professor Gey pejoratively labels as "unquestioned truths."

I say "pejorative," since it seems to me that when Gey writes of citizens who believe in these "unquestioned truths," he is claiming that they do so irrationally or without adequate warrant. But this is surely not the case, for two reasons: (1) There are numerous well-reasoned works critical of the sort of crude relativism Gey offers, and none of these works presents esoteric religious arguments whose premises would seem controversial to many unbelievers.[32] (2) Gey does not interact with any of the relevant academic literature on religious belief, morality and rationality. Thus, it is difficult to know how he would reply to the sophisticated and compelling arguments offered by members of the growing intellectual movement of theistic philosophers in Anglo-American philosophy published before 1990 (the year Gey's article appeared in print).[33]

In fact in chapter five, I argue that the existence of God best accounts for the moral intuitions that seem to ground our understanding of natural moral law and natural rights, principles without which liberal democracy seems to lose its point.

As America moved into the twentieth century, separationism was increasingly perceived as *the* American understanding of the establishment clause. Among its most vocal and public advocates were Baptists, Freemasons, the Ku Klux Klan, nativists and secularists. One of the most ardent separationists of the twentieth century, Supreme Court Justice Hugo Black, was a Baptist and Freemason and, up until a little over

---

[32]See, for example, the works cited in note 30.
[33]See, for example, Richard Swinburne, *The Existence of God* (New York: Oxford University Press, 1979); Richard Swinburne, *Faith & Reason* (Oxford: Clarendon, 1983); Alvin Plantinga and Nicholas Wolterstorff, eds., *Faith & Rationality: Reason & Belief in God* (Notre Dame, Ind.: University of Notre Dame Press, 1983); William Lane Craig, *The Kalam Cosmological Argument* (New York: Macmillan, 1979); Alvin Plantinga, *God and Other Minds: A Study of the Rational Justification of Belief in God* (Ithaca, N.Y.: Cornell University Press, 1967); J. P. Moreland, *Scaling the Secular City: A Defense of Christianity* (Grand Rapids: Baker, 1987); John Finnis, *Natural Law and Natural Rights* (Oxford: Clarendon, 1980); John Finnis, *Fundamentals of Ethics* (Washington, D.C.: Georgetown University Press, 1983); Mortimer Adler, *Ten Philosophical Mistakes* (New York: Macmillan, 1985); Mortimer Adler, *How to Think About God: A Guide For the 20th Century Pagan* (New York: Macmillan, 1980).

a decade before his 1937 nomination to the Court, a member of the Ku Klux Klan. Although, as Hamburger points out, Black "in later years would discount his association with the Invisible Empire of the Ku Klux Klan" as an innocent membership in a fraternal organization, "Black's account of his participating in the Klan was, at best, understated."[34] Hamburger presents a detailed history of Black's Klan affiliation, which leaves no doubt that Black was no nominal Klansman who wore his sheets only on holidays and for weddings.[35] According to Hamburger, "in September 1923 Black joined the powerful Richard E. Lee Klan No. 1 and promptly became Kladd of his Klavern—the officer who initiated new members by administering the oath about 'white supremacy' and 'separation of church and state.'"[36] Apparently, to quote the comedian Dennis Miller, Black was "burning the cross at both ends."[37]

By the time the U.S. Supreme Court applied the establishment clause to the states in the 1947 *Everson* case, the separationist understanding was so widely accepted throughout the country that the Court could make it a fixed point in constitutional law without needing anything like the Blaine amendment. And the Court did so in *Everson*, whose majority opinion was penned by Justice Black. The case concerned whether or not the Township of Ewing's payment to parents for busing their children to Catholic parochial schools violated the establishment clause. Black concluded that it did not, for three reasons: the payment was not given directly to a religious organization; it was available to children in all schools including nonreligious private schools; and it was much like other services such as police, fire department, etc. Although many of Black's separationist allies both off and on the Court (four Supreme Court justices dissented) did not like the fact that the wrong party, Township of Ewing, won the lawsuit, they would realize in coming years that Black had delicately and cleverly placed into the arsenal of constitutional

---

[34]Hamburger, *Separation of Church and State*, pp. 423-24.

[35]Ibid., pp. 422-34.

[36]Ibid., p. 426.

[37]Joe Kovacs, "Dennis Miller Jabs Democrat All-Stars," WorldNewsDaily.com (September 10, 2003) <www.worldnetdaily.com/news/article.asp?ARTICLE_ID=34524>. Miller was talking about Senator Robert Byrd (D-WV), another former member of the Ku Klux Klan.

law adjudication—for the first time—the principles of separationism. Black writes in Everson:

> The "establishment of religion" clause of the First Amendment means at least this: Neither a state nor the Federal Government can set up a church. Neither can pass laws which aid one religion, aid all religions, or prefer one religion over another. Neither can force nor influence a person to go to or to remain away from church against his will or force him to profess a belief or disbelief in any religion. No person can be punished for entertaining or professing religious beliefs or disbeliefs, for church attendance or non-attendance. No tax in any amount, large or small, can be levied to support any religious activities or institutions, whatever they may be called, or whatever form they may adopt to teach or practice religion. Neither a state nor the Federal Government can, openly or secretly, participate in the affairs of any religious organizations or groups and vice versa. In the words of Jefferson, the clause against establishment of religion by law was intended to erect "a wall of separation between Church and State."[38]

Hamburger writes that Black "understood what he was doing." For "only ten years before, when Black was appointed to the Court, Catholics vociferously condemned him for his Klan membership." What the facts and circumstances of *Everson* afforded him was "an opportunity to make separation the unanimous standard of the Court while reaching a judgment that would undercut Catholic criticism."[39] A fellow Baptist and separationist ally of Black's, the Reverend Joseph Martin Dawson, began to understand this as well. Thus, in commenting on the Everson case in his autobiography, he wrote, "We had lost a battle, but won the war!"[40]

Despite this victory and a few subsequent ones for the strong

---

[38]*Everson v. Board of Education*, 330 U.S. 15-16 (1947). The citation from *Reynolds v. United States* has been omitted from this quote.

[39]Hamburger, *Separation*, p. 462.

[40]Joseph Martin Dawson, *A Thousand Months to Remember: An Autobiography* (Waco, Tex.: Baylor University Press, 1964), p. 194. This sentence is also quoted by Hamburger, *Separation*, p. 462. It should be noted that the Rev. Dawson never shared Justice Black's affection for the Klan. In fact, Dawson was a courageous opponent of racial prejudice. See Dawson, *A Thousand Months*, p. 165. See also James M. Dunn, *The Ethical Thought of Joseph Martin Dawson* (Th.D. diss., Southwestern Baptist Theological Seminary, 1966), pp. 151-86.

separationists,[41] the Supreme Court has not fully absorbed the premises of their jurisprudence. In fact, the contemporary Court seems to be moving in a direction more accommodating of religion, especially in the areas of religious speech and public funding of schools when the funds are directed to the schools by private choice or when there is no evidence that the funds are being used for indoctrination.[42]

Exceptions to this are free-exercise cases involving states in which there are Blaine-like laws.[43] For example, the Supreme Court, in *Locke v. Davey* (2004),[44] refused to overturn the state of Washington's Blaine-like amendment on free-exercise grounds. The amendment reads: "No public money or property shall be appropriated for or applied to any religious worship, exercise or instruction, or the support of any religious

---

[41]See, for example, and *Aquilar v. Felton*, 473 U.S. 402 (1985). The Court held as violating the establishment clause, because of excessive entanglement, New York City's use of federal funds to help underprivileged children who attended parochial schools and were in need of remedial reading and math; the program involved the use of public-school teachers in those schools, while banning religious symbols from their classrooms and religious indoctrination in their lessons. Issued the same day as *Aguilar*, *School District of Grand Rapids v. Ball*, 473 U.S. 373 (1985) concerned similar issues that led the Court to strike down two school district programs on establishment-clause grounds based on excessive entanglement.

[42]See, for example, the following: *Widmer v. Vincent*, 454 U.S. 263 (1981), where the Court found that a religious student group's free speech and association rights were violated when it was prohibited by a state university from meeting on campus. In *Lamb's Chapel v. Center Moriches Union Free School District*, 508 U.S. 384 (1993), the Court ruled no violation of the establishment clause occurred when a public school district permitted a church to show, after school hours and on school property, a religiously-oriented film on family life. In *Zobrest v. Catalina*, 113 U.S. 2462 (1993), the Court ruled that a school district may not refuse to supply a sign language interpreter to a student at a religious high school when such government benefits are neutrally dispensed to students without regard to the public-nonpublic or sectarian-nonsectarian nature of the school. In *Capitol Square Review Board v. Pinette*, 515 U.S. 753 (1995), the Court found that it was content-based discrimination for the government to prohibit a controversial organization from sponsoring a religious display in a public park. In *Rosenberger v. The University of Virginia*, 515 U.S 819 (1995), the Court ruled that it was a denial of college students' free speech rights, as well as a risk of nurturing hostility toward religion, to prohibit the students from using student funds for a religiously oriented publication. In *Mitchell v. Helms*, 530 U.S. 793 (2000), the Court found that direct funding to private schools, including religious schools, does not violate the establishment clause, since the distribution is evenhanded and the use of the money to indoctrinate in religious schools cannot reasonably be attributed to government. In *Mitchell*, 530 U.S. 836 (2000) (O'Connor, J., concurring), Justice O'Connor found that direct funding to private schools, including religious schools, does not violate the establishment clause, since the distribution is evenhanded *and* there is no evidence that funds given to religious schools was used to indoctrinate.

[43]See *Locke v. Davey*, 538 U.S. 1031 (2004) and *Witters v. Commission for the Blind* 112 Wash. 2d 363, 771 P. 2d 1119 (1989).

[44]*Locke*, 538 U.S. 1031.

establishment."[45] The case concerned Joshua Davey, a theology student who qualified for a state scholarship but was denied it on the grounds that Washington law forbade any funding for theological education even though similarly situated students majoring in philosophy, history, religion or chemistry could make use of the same financial help if offered it. The Court held that states have much leeway in the area of funding, and thus Washington could have a Blaine-like law without violating Mr. Davey's free-exercise rights. The flip side of this leeway, however, was that if Washington had funded Davey's theology education, it would not have violated the establishment clause. So contrary to the conventional wisdom and some strong separationist groups, *Locke v. Davey* was not a victory for strong separationism.

TAKING RELIGION SERIOUSLY

By making a convincing case that there are good historical and textual reasons not to equate strong separationism with antiestablishment, Hamburger has provided a conceptual scheme by which courts may affirm the constitutionality of laws that are tied to religious understandings but are nevertheless not "state establishments." That is, a government within the United States may pass laws that provide public approval and sustenance to moral understandings that are consistent with, congenial to or have their grounding in certain religious traditions but, nevertheless, are thought by some citizens to advance the public good. Although not in line with the agenda of many contemporary separationists, this concept would have been well-received by their anti-establishment predecessors, such as the Danbury Baptists, who believed in the importance of religion and morality in the preservation of a constitutional republic. As Daniel Dreisbach notes:

> Although no friend of religious establishments, many evangelical dissenters resisted efforts to inhibit religion's ability to influence public life and culture, to deprive religious leaders of the civil liberty to participate in politics armed with political opinions informed by religious values,

---

[45]Washington Constitution, art. 1, sec. 11.

and to restrain the freedom of churches to define and advance their own mission and ministries, whether spiritual, social, or civic.[46]

In order to appreciate the contrast between contemporary strong separationism and the views held by eighteenth- and nineteenth-century dissenters, consider the current debate over abortion. Many strong separationists support abortion rights on antiestablishment and/or free-exercise grounds.[47] They argue that the prolife position on abortion—that the fetus is a full-fledged member of the human community and thus a subject of rights from the moment of conception—depends on a religious metaphysics. Writes Paul Simmons, a defender of this point of view:

> The fact that many people believe strongly that a zygote is a person is by now well established. The First Amendment allows people to believe as they will as a matter of conscience or religious belief. That is a matter of freedom of religion. But as a definition of personhood for constitutional protections in a pluralistic society, the zygote-as-person rationale is untenable in the extreme. . . . Abstract metaphysical speculation has its rightful place in theology; but it must finally be rejected as inappropriate to the logic necessary for democratic rule.[48]

---

[46]Daniel L. Dreisbach, *Thomas Jefferson and the Wall of Separation Between Church and State* (New York: New York University Press, 2002), p. 52. Concerning the era in which President Jefferson penned his letter to the Danbury Baptists, Hamburger writes: "In all probability . . . only a handful of Baptists, if any, and no Baptist organizations made separation their demand. Instead Baptists focused on other, more traditional, claims of religious liberty. What Baptists sought not only differed from separation of church and state but also conflicted with it. Tactically, dissenters could not afford to demand separation, for a potent argument against them had been that they denied the connection between religion and government—a serious charge in a society in which religion was widely understood to be the necessary foundation of morality and government" (Hamburger, *Separation*, pp. 177-78).

[47]See, e.g., Peter S. Wenz, *Abortion Rights as Religious Freedom* (Philadelphia: Temple University Press, 1992); Simmons, "Religious Liberty and Abortion Policy"; Paul D. Simmons, "Religious Liberty and the Abortion Debate," *Journal of Church and State* 32, no. 3 (Summer 1990): 567-84; Stuart Rosenbaum, "Abortion, the Constitution, and Metaphysics," *Journal of Church and State* 43, no. 4 (Autumn 2001): 707-23; Judith Jarvis Thomson, "Abortion," *Boston Review* 20, no. 3 (Summer 1995): 11-15. For responses to this point of view, see Francis J. Beckwith, "Law, Religion and the Metaphysics of Abortion: A Reply to Simmons" *Journal of Church and State* 43, no. 1 (Winter 2001): 19-33; Francis J. Beckwith, "When You Come to a Fork in the Road, Take It? Abortion, Personhood, and the Jurisprudence of Neutrality," *Journal of Church and State* 45, no. 3 (Summer 2003): 485-97; Francis J. Beckwith, "Thomson's 'Equal Reasonableness' Argument for Abortion Rights: A Critique," *American Journal of Jurisprudence* 49 (2004): 185-98.

[48]Simmons, "Religious Liberty and Abortion Policy," p. 75.

Therefore, any law that prohibits abortion on those grounds would establish religion (thus violating the establishment clause) and/or impede the free exercise of women whose religious beliefs may permit them to obtain an abortion because the fetus is not a subject of rights (thus violating the free-exercise clause).

Of course, it is no coincidence that opponents of abortion are generally more religious than those who support abortion rights.[49] Abortion opponents usually accept a view of the nature of the unborn that is consistent with their religion's view of human nature.[50] However, those who offer this point of view in the public square do not merely stipulate the veracity of their position, as one would expect from people whose purpose is to simply propound dogmas to condemn the "infidels."[51] Rather, they offer arguments that consist of reasons that are remarkably public. They do not extract their reasons uncritically from a religious text or from the pronouncements of a religious authority, and their arguments are fully accessible to even those who dispute their veracity and/or the conclusions for which these reasons are conscripted.

Sophisticated prolife advocates typically argue from the nature of the unborn in order to establish the standing of each unborn person as a rights-bearer who ought to be protected by our laws. This type of argument is meant to rebut the typical abortion-choice argument that locates a human being's intrinsic value with whether it is presently able to exercise or exhibit certain functions, for example, consciousness,

---

[49]There are, of course, exceptions. For example, Doris Gordon (president, Libertarians for Life) and Nat Hentoff (writer, *The Village Voice*) are prolife atheists. As far as I know, it is Doris Gordon who coined the term "abortion-choice," which I use in this chapter and elsewhere. See her introductory essay in *International Journal of Sociology and Social Policy* 19, no. 3/4 (1999).

[50]See, e.g., Patrick Lee, *Abortion and Unborn Human Life* (Washington, D.C.: Catholic University of America Press, 1996); J. P. Moreland and Scott B. Rae, *Body and Soul: Human Nature and the Crisis in Ethics* (Downers Grove, Ill.: InterVarsity Press, 2000); Francis J. Beckwith, *Defending Life: A Moral and Legal Case Against Abortion Choice* (New York: Cambridge University Press, 2007); Robert P. George (with Alfonso Gomez-Lobo), "Statement of Professor George," in *Human Cloning and Human Dignity: An Ethical Inquiry* (Washington, D.C.: President's Council on Bioethics, 2002).

[51]This is the stereotype advanced by Simmons when he writes that the prolife view of the unborn's intrinsic value is *merely* a claim of "Catholic dogma" and/or "special knowledge" that is neither "subject to critical analysis" nor rooted in "reason" (Simmons, "Religious Liberty and Abortion Policy," pp. 75, 72, 71, 71).

self-awareness, ability to communicate, possession of a self-concept.[52]
In a nutshell, prolifers respond to this sort of argument by arguing that
there is a deep connection between our human nature and the rights
that spring from it, which a just government is obligated to recognize.
Because the unborn—from zygote to blastocyst to embryo to fetus—is
the same being, the same substance, that develops into an adult, the
actualization of a human being's potential—that is, "human" appearance and the exercise of rational and moral powers as an adult (which
abortion-choice advocates argue determine a person's intrinsic value)—
is merely the public presentation of functions latent in every human
substance, from the moment it is brought into being. A human may
lose and regain those functions throughout her life, but the substance
remains the same being. Moreover, if one's value is conditioned on
certain accidental properties, then the human equality presupposed by
our legal institutions and our form of government—the philosophical
foundation of our constitutional regime—is a fiction. In that case our
government has no principled basis for rejecting the notion that human rights ought to be distributed to individuals on the basis of native
intellectual abilities or other value-giving properties, such as rationality or self-awareness. One can only reject this notion by affirming that
human beings are intrinsically valuable because they possess a particular nature from the moment they come into existence. That is to say,
what individual human beings are, and not what they do, makes them
subjects of rights.

It is not surprising, therefore, that supporters of abortion rights rebut
the prolife case by offering their own philosophical anthropology. That
is, they present arguments to show that the unborn, though human beings, do not possess the requisite characteristics that require the government to protect them as subjects of rights.[53]

Both the prolifer and the abortion rights advocate offer contrary accounts of the same being, the unborn. The former offers an account of
the human person that is at home in a certain type of religious world-

---

[52]See, e.g., David Boonin, *A Defense of Abortion* (New York: Cambridge University Press, 2002);
Michael Tooley, *Abortion and Infanticide* (New York: Oxford University Press, 1983).
[53]See Boonin, *A Defense of Abortion;* Tooley, *Abortion and Infanticide.*

view, though it is certainly not unreasonable to accept the prolife position while rejecting the religious tradition from which it sprang.[54] On the other hand, the abortion-choice advocate offers an account of the human person that denies the soundness of the prolife position. Although the abortion-choice position or some modest form of it is embraced by some Christian citizens,[55] most of its advocates embrace a worldview tradition whose philosophical and theological commitments claim to be "secular" and harbor an antipathy to the influence of traditional religion on public life. For example, the number of organizations and individuals that own websites advancing a secular worldview while supporting church-state separation and the abortion-choice position are nearly limitless.[56]

So both the prolifer and the abortion-choice advocate present contrary answers to the same question: who and what are we? Yet, according to the separationist, only the prolifer is forbidden from shaping public policy because her point of view is "[a]bstract metaphysical speculation [that] has its rightful place in theology; but . . . [should be] rejected as inappropriate to the logic necessary for democratic rule."[57] But the abortion-choice advocate attempts to justify his position by offering a different metaphysical account, one that picks out certain presently exercisable abilities or functions that a being must have in order to be

---

[54]See note 50.

[55]See, for example, Paul D. Simmons "Personhood, the Bible, and the Abortion Debate," Religious Coalition for Reproductive Choice Educational Series, No. 3 <www.rcrc.org/pdf/RCRC_EdSeries_Personhood.pdf>; and Virginia Ramey Mollenkott, "Respecting the Moral Agency of Women," Religious Coalition for Reproductive Choice Educational Series, No. 1 <www.rcrc.org/pdf/moral_agency_women.pdf>.

[56]For example, Debra Arias writes, "I did what I could to support pro-choice . . . because this was the only area of my life that I felt the radical right threatened. I was wrong" (Debra Arias, "A Close Encounter with the Religious Right," Separation of Church and State home page <http://candst.tripod.com/tnppage/debbie.htm>). Another example is the Americans United website, which urged, "We encourage all AU activists to join us in marching behind our church-state separation banner. AU Executive Director Barry Lynn will be one of the featured speakers at the rally" ("AU Joins 'March for Women's Lives' - Sunday, April 25" online posting [April 20, 2004] The Wall of Separation: Official Weblog of Au.org <http://blog.au.org/2004/04/20/march_for_women/>). A final example is from the Council for Secular Humanism's page, "Mature adults should be allowed to fulfill their aspirations, to express their sexual preferences, to exercise reproductive freedom . . ." (The Affirmations of Humanism: A Statement of Principles, Council for Secular Humanism <www.secularhumanism.org/index.php?section=main&page=affirmations>).

[57]Simmons, "Religious Liberty and Abortion Policy," p. 75.

accorded the protections of our laws. There seems to be no good reason, except a type of crass philosophical apartheid that would justify saying that this prochoice account has its rightful place in politics and law while it's alternative, the prolife view, "has its rightful place in theology."[58]

This unjustified public marginalization of citizens who have a religious understanding of certain political and moral issues results when one interprets antiestablishment as equivalent to a total separation of religion from our political and legal institutions. As Hamburger and others point out, the Danbury Baptists and most other dissenters did not understand antiestablishment in this way,[59] and neither should we. The courts should not be in the business of siding with a militant secularism that seeks to have its metaphysics and morals firmly embedded in our laws while it suggests that the metaphysics and morals of its religious opponents, regardless of the quality of the arguments offered, should not even be considered by the citizenry simply because they flow from a religious worldview. If liberal democracy means anything, it should at least mean that all citizens—regardless of the religious or nonreligious source of their policy proposals—should be allowed to offer their best public arguments without first being required by the courts or secularists to undergo a metaphysical litmus test.[60]

ARE THERE LIMITS TO RELIGIOUS FREE EXERCISE?

It is obvious that religious freedom is one of the fundamental liberties in American constitutional jurisprudence. But are there limits to this liberty? Should, for example, fundamentalist Mormons receive the state's imprimatur for their polygamous unions? Ought the government to allow Muslim citizens to operate under Shari'a law, or Christian theonomists under "biblical law"? Should these groups be allowed to operate contrary to, or independent of, the law of the land?

Present free-exercise jurisprudence. It is important to recognize that

---

[58]Ibid.

[59]See note 46.

[60]For an extended defense of a similar point of view, see Nicholas Wolterstorff's contribution to Robert Audi and Nicholas Wolterstorff, *Religion in the Public Square* (Lanham, Md.: Rowman & Littlefield, 1997).

some laws in fact include exemptions. For example, soon after the Supreme Court in 1990 denied the right of Native American religionists in Oregon to be exempted from the state's narcotics laws that prohibited the smoking of peyote *(Employment Division v. Smith)*,[61] the state legislature changed its drug laws to include a religious exemption. In addition, the Supreme Court has allowed religious exemptions to generally applicable laws. For example, in the 1972 case of *Wisconsin v. Yoder*,[62] the Court, employing the free-exercise clause, carved out an exemption to the state's mandatory school attendance law and allowed Amish students to opt out after eighth grade. The Court reasoned that, since the Amish community has a stellar record of rearing its children, the state had to prove that it had a compelling interest in abridging the free-exercise rights of Amish parents. The Court concluded that Wisconsin failed to meet this burden.

In *Yoder*, the burden was on the state to provide really good reasons for not allowing the Amish to educate their children in a way that was consistent with their own religious tradition. In *Smith*, the Court shifted the burden from the state to the person who was suing the state. So, all the state had to show in *Smith* was that its law is generally applicable (i.e., it applies to all citizens similarly situated) and neutral (i.e., it does not single out or target a specific religious practice). The fact that the law impeded a group's religious liberty was an incidental result of the law, and thus the law could not be declared unconstitutional simply for that reason.

So under the Court's current understanding of religious free exercise, as long as a law is generally applicable and neutral, all the state needs is a rational basis (i.e., any remotely plausible reason) for a law that forbids or limits the practices of religious polygamists, theonomists, Muslims committed to Shari'a and others.

Is free exercise a dead letter? The problem with this understanding is that it seems to make the free-exercise clause a dead letter. That is, with the exception of a blatant case of the government targeting a religion,[63]

---

[61]*Employment Division v. Smith*, 494 U.S. 872 (1990).

[62]*Wisconsin v. Yoder*, 406 U.S. 205 (1972).

[63]See, for example, *Church of the Lukumi Babalu Aye v. City of Hialeah*, 508 U.S. 520 (1993).

a jurist can never effectively employ the free-exercise clause to overturn generally applicable laws that are neutral but nevertheless limit or totally inhibit a citizen's religious free exercise. Although many citizens think that the government ought not to permit polygamists, theonomists or Muslims in favor of Shari'a law to have their own legal system that is parallel to and not under the authority of U.S. or state law, they do think that the government should have a greater burden in justifying its laws if those laws encumber one's religious free exercise.

Take, for example, the 2004 California Supreme Court case of *Catholic Charities v. State of California Department of Managed Health Care.*[64] Under California's Women's Contraception Equity Act (WCEA), all employers in the state that offer their employees coverage for prescription drugs must also provide coverage for contraceptives. Because Catholic moral theology forbids the use of artificial contraception, Catholic Charities (CC) did not want to provide contraceptive coverage as part of its prescription drug coverage. Even though the law allowed for "religious exemptions," the exemptions were defined in such a way that they did not protect organizations like CC. These groups are religious in their origin, affiliation and mission, but fall outside the scope of these exemptions because they employ and provide care for many outside their faith and do not engage in evangelism or preaching. When before the California Supreme Court, CC argued, among other things, that these exemptions were written in such a way that CC's free exercise rights were violated because it defined what counted as state-defined religious practice for CC and similar groups. Appealing to *Smith*, the court rejected CC's case and ruled that the organization had to provide its employees with "benefits" that are used for purposes that CC's moral theology teaches are sinful.

The sole dissenter was Justice Janice Rogers Brown, who left the California Supreme Court in 2005 to be a federal judge on the U.S. Court of Appeals for the District of Columbia. She offers this blistering analysis:

---

[64]*Catholic Charities v. State of California Department of Managed Health Care*, 32 Cal. 4d 527 (2004).

Here we are dealing with an intentional, purposeful intrusion into a religious organization's expression of its religious tenets and sense of mission. The government is not accidentally or incidentally interfering with religious practice; it is doing so willfully by making a judgment about what is or is not religious. This is precisely the sort of behavior that has been condemned in every other context. The conduct is hardly less offensive because it is codified. . . . This is such a crabbed and constricted view of religion that it would define the ministry of Jesus Christ as a secular activity.[65]

Here's the problem: how do we protect the religious liberty of groups like Catholic Charities while allowing the government to pass apparently good laws that do restrict the religious practices of others? I believe that the answer lies in the American Founders' understanding of religious free exercise.

The founders, free exercise and limits to free exercise. America's Founders were wise enough to understand that religious freedom could not be limitless. They also understood that this precious liberty could not be restricted unless the state could provide exceptionally good justification for legal restrictions. This is why the wording of free-exercise provisions in state constitutions at the time of the American founding typically allowed for the limitation of religious liberty if the prohibited actions would interfere with some aspect of the community's good. New York state's Constitution (1777) is typical in this regard:

And whereas we are required, by the benevolent principles of rational liberty, not only to expel civil tyranny, but also to guard against that spiritual oppression and intolerance wherewith the bigotry and ambition of weak and wicked priests and princes have scourged mankind, this convention doth further, in the name and by the authority of the good people of this State, ordain, determine, and declare, that the free exercise and enjoyment of religious profession and worship, without discrimination or preference, shall forever hereafter be allowed, within this State, to all mankind: Provided, That the liberty of conscience, hereby granted, shall not be so construed as to excuse acts of licentiousness, or justify practices inconsistent with the peace or safety of this State.[66]

---

[65]*Catholic Charities*, 32 Cal 4d 578, 583 (Brown, J., dissenting).
[66]New York Constitution, art. 38.

The reasoning is similar to what the Supreme Court employed in 1878 when it rejected the argument of Mormons that the free-exercise clause protected their religious practice of plural marriage. In 1862, the U.S. Congress had passed the first of several antipolygamy statutes for the purpose of stopping the growing population of practicing Mormon polygamists in Utah. Because Utah was a U.S. territory at the time, the federal government had jurisdiction over Utah, and thus the First Amendment of the federal Constitution could be applied to the anti-polygamy statutes. (Today, because of the doctrine of incorporation, it would not matter whether it was a state or federal statute.)

In *Reynolds v. United States* (1878) the Court rejected the Mormons' free exercise argument on the grounds that even though "Congress was deprived of all legislative power over mere opinion, . . . [it] was left free to reach actions [such as polygamy] which were in violation of social duties or subversive of good order."[67] As noted in chapter one, what the Court meant by this is that certain institutions and ways of life, such as marriage and the family, are essential to the preservation of civil society. For this reason, the government may craft its laws in such a way that certain practices receive a privileged position in our social fabric, and actions contrary to them should be prohibited or at least discouraged even if they have religious sanction.

On the other hand, the common good is undermined when citizens are forced to choose between obeying the law and engaging in their religious practices when those practices do not undermine, and may very well advance, the public good. For example, when the Supreme Court in *Yoder* gave a free-exercise exemption to the Amish, the public good was advanced. However, when Catholic Charities was forced by the California Supreme Court to pay for its employees' contraceptive use, CC was literally required to underwrite sexual practices that are overtly hostile to its own theological understanding, an understanding that is integral to a well-established tradition in moral philosophy. This ruling runs counter to the common good.

In my view, the courts should return to the reasoning of the Found-

---

[67]*Reynolds v. United States*, 98 U.S. 145, 164 (1878).

ers. Their reasoning allows for the widest possible religious free exercise consistent with preserving and protecting the public good. This, of course, will not eliminate debates on controversial questions over which reasonable citizens disagree. What it will do is provide us with a conceptual framework that puts teeth back into the free-exercise clause.

CONCLUSION

The First Amendment's protection of religious liberty and its prohibition of religious establishment have been applied recently in ways that seem inconsistent with religious liberty and serve to privilege secular beliefs on controversial moral and social issues. Serious Christians, regardless of their partisan affiliations, should be concerned about this.

In the conclusion to his book, Philip Hamburger writes that because "Americans . . . gradually forgot the character of their old, antiestablishment religious liberty," they "eventually came to understand their religious freedom as a separation of church and state."[68] Thus, despite its widespread acceptance, it lacks constitutional authority. For this reason and because of its roots in prejudice, "the idea of separation should, at best, be viewed with suspicion."[69]

On the other hand, Christians should also be careful not to marginalize the voices of non-Christians and thus commit the same harm as secularists have committed against Christians. If Christians in a liberal democracy believe in religious liberty and religious disestablishment, they must be conscientious in making sure that the liberties they want to enjoy are extended equitably to all citizens, even those who do not share their faith.

---

[68]Hamburger, *Separation*, p. 492.
[69]Ibid., p. 483.

4

Secular Liberalism
and the Neutral State

Many Christians have been critical of what they believe are the excesses of some of the cultural beliefs and practices that have arisen out of liberal democracies. These excesses include the proliferation of obscenity, the vulgarity of public discourse, the application of the free-market philosophy to personal and family life, the prevalence of abortion, the increasing acceptance of homosexual practice, the disintegration of the family, the commodification of the human body (especially of the unborn), the application of politically correct policies that marginalize serious religious believers on university and college campuses, and the use of taxpayer-funded public schools to teach messages inconsistent with the moral and religious traditions of the home.

In order to resist what these citizens believe are deleterious trends in our culture and social fabric, they have become more politically active and have, in some cases, tried to shape the laws of their communities. Nevertheless, these Christians are also strong supporters of liberal democracy as a political system. For this reason, in their critiques they often argue that what they see as the cultural decay and marginalization of traditional and religious voices are not necessary consequences of liberal democracy. Rather, they argue that elite culture—in politics, law, entertainment and education—has uncritically embraced a point of view that some call secular liberalism. It is a view often presented by its advocates as necessary for liberal democracy, even though it seems to require the state to exclude the voices of religious citizens from shaping public policy. In this chapter, we will look carefully at this dispute. We will first define secular liberalism and then critically assess three arguments for it. I will conclude that secular liberalism is a flawed position and that its employment in politics is likely to diminish rather than advance the liberty of Christian citizens.

SECULAR LIBERALISM

In opposition to Christian activism, some argue that if the views of Christian citizens were to become enshrined in our law, it would violate a fundamental principle of liberal democracy: in a pluralist society that includes citizens with conflicting and contrary philosophical and religious beliefs, the law should not embrace any one of these perspectives as correct.[1] Some argue that this principle is supported by America's tradition of church-state separation that supposedly bars legislators, through the U.S. Constitution's free exercise and establishment clauses, from imposing a religious view of the human person and the common good on citizens who disagree with that view.[2]

This position is called secular liberalism for two conjoined reasons. It is *liberal* insofar as its proponents claim that, because all citizens should be treated with equal regard, the resolution of moral disputes should be left to the individual rights-bearing citizen who has a fundamental right to be emancipated from all external restraints in order to properly exercise his liberty under the direction of his own freely chosen view of the good life. This means that the state has an obligation to ensure that adult citizens should be free to pursue whatever they believe is good for them without the constraints of family, church or other citizens' objections, etc. So if a citizen wants to have an abortion, procure physician-assisted suicide or live in a sexual relationship with multiple partners, the state has no interest in forbidding or strongly con-

---

[1]See, for example, Ronald Dworkin, *Life's Dominion: An Argument About Abortion, Euthanasia, and Individual Freedom* (New York: Random House, 1993); John Rawls, *Political Liberalism*, 2nd ed. (New York: Columbia University Press, 1996); Judith Jarvis Thomson, "Abortion," *Boston Review* 20, no. 3 (Summer 1995): 11-15 <http://bostonreview.mit.edu/BR20.3/thomson.html>. All references to Thomson's piece in this chapter are from the online version.

[2]See, for example, Paul D. Simmons, "Religious Liberty and Abortion Policy: *Casey* as 'Catch-22,'" *Journal of Church and State* 42, no. 1 (Winter 2000): 69-88; and Paul D. Simmons, "Religious Liberty and the Abortion Debate," *Journal of Church and State* 32, no. 3 (Summer 1990): 567-84.

demning these behaviors as long as all the participants consent and no third parties are coerced or harmed. This perspective is also *secular*, for it requires that the only permissible external restraints that may be placed on citizens are those that are both not dependent on a religious worldview and help ensure that the unencumbered rights-bearing citizen exercise his liberty without being interfered with and without interfering with the same liberty held by others. This means that if the state is going to limit the citizen's liberty it must be for a nonreligious reason that enhances everyone's liberty. So the state may discourage sexual promiscuity but only because it may spread disease and unwanted pregnancy. However, as long as all the participants consent and they are all employing protection, it is none of the state's business. The state may also subsidize the free acts of poor people. So in the name of advancing liberty, the state may help pay for the abortions of poor women. But under no circumstances may the state obstruct a citizen's liberty just because the citizen's acts are immoral or undermine the common good. For, according to the secular liberal, such considerations rely on controversial beliefs (often religious ones) that are not shared by some, if not most, citizens.

Secular liberalism (SL) is widely held in different forms by an array of thinkers across the religious and political spectrum. For this reason, secular liberalism should not be confused with the popular political philosophy known as "liberalism," which is associated with left-leaning members of the Democratic Party in the United States or the Labour Party in the United Kingdom. Some of the strongest critics of SL are self-described liberals, such as William Galston[3] and Michael Sandel.[4] On the other hand, some of the strongest supporters of secular liberalism (at least on the matter of the role of religious worldviews in the public square) are non-liberals such as Episcopal priest and former Republican U.S. Senator John Danforth (Missouri)[5] and conservative po-

---

[3]William Galston, *Liberal Purposes: Goods, Virtues, and Diversity in the Liberal State* (New York: Cambridge University Press, 1991).

[4]Michael Sandel, *Democracy's Discontent: America in Search of a Public Philosophy* (Cambridge, Mass.: Harvard University Press, 1996).

[5]John Danforth, *Faith and Politics: How the "Moral Values" Debate Divides America and How to Move Forward Together* (New York: Penguin, 2006).

litical commentator Andrew Sullivan, a self-described "gay Catholic."[6]

Secular liberalism has had a tremendous impact on the law and the way in which courts (especially the Supreme Court) have dealt with social issues such as abortion and homosexual conduct. For example, in the famous case declaring abortion a constitutional right, *Roe v. Wade*, Justice Harry Blackmun writes in his majority opinion: "We need not resolve the difficult question of when life begins. When those trained in the respective disciplines of medicine, philosophy, and theology are unable to arrive at any consensus, the judiciary, at this point in the development of man's knowledge, is not in a position to speculate."[7]

According to secular liberalism, because reasonable people disagree on fundamental questions of the nature of reality, knowledge, human beings and the good life, the state ought not to embrace any one of these views as correct. Its more sophisticated proponents include legal theorist Ronald Dworkin[8] (1931-) and the late philosopher John Rawls (1921-2002),[9] both of whom have offered important political theories in order to defend a political regime in which there is wide philosophical and religious disagreement among its citizens and yet a justified system of laws that does not collapse into moral relativism. As understood and embraced in popular culture, secular liberalism accentuates the fact of pluralism, that there exists a plurality of different and contrary opinions on matters religious, philosophical and moral. From this fact, many in our culture conclude that one cannot say with any confidence that anyone's view on religious, philosophical or moral matters is better than anyone else's view. Given that, it is a mistake to claim that one's religious, philosophical or moral beliefs are exclusively correct and that fellow citizens in other religious, philosophical and moral traditions, no matter how sincere or devoted, hold false beliefs. Thus, it is wrong to hold that political or moral positions derived from one's reli-

---

[6]Andrew Sullivan, *The Conservative Soul: How We Lost It, How to Get It Back* (San Francisco: HarperCollins, 2006).

[7]*Roe v. Wade*, 410 U.S. 113, 160 (1973).

[8]Ronald Dworkin, *Sovereign Virtue: The Theory and Practice of Equality* (Cambridge, Mass.: Harvard University Press, 2000).

[9]Rawls, *Political Liberalism*.

gious, philosophical or moral tradition ought to be the proper subject of laws that constrain another's liberty.

THREE ARGUMENTS FOR SECULAR LIBERALISM

Although secular liberalism is offered by its proponents as the most rational ordering of the public square in a society in which its citizens embrace conflicting and contrary worldviews, I think there are good reasons to believe that it cannot succeed in this noble purpose. In order to support this conclusion, we will look at three arguments that are often employed to defend secular liberalism: (A) the golden-rule-contract argument, (B) the secular reason argument and (C) the err-on-the-side-of-liberty argument.

It is, however, important to understand what we are not trying to accomplish in this chapter. We are not examining the positions held by certain Christian citizens and arguing that they are better than their rivals. Our purpose in this chapter is simply to address three arguments that are employed to prohibit, in principle, legislation informed by religious thought (including Christian theology). Of course, even if you conclude that these three arguments for secular liberalism fail, it may be the case that the Christians' arguments for their political positions nevertheless fail on their own merits. But that is not the focus of this chapter. What we are examining is the question of whether liberal democracy itself forbids these Christians from ever making their case in the public square and/or having their views enshrined in law.

The golden-rule-contract argument. Philosopher Robert Audi has argued in various works that religious citizens ought not employ the power of the state to pass legislation that would coerce disagreeing citizens to act in accordance with that legislation, for the religious citizens would not want the disagreeing citizen to do the same to them. Writes Audi, "[It] is a kind of restraint I would wish to be observed by members of other religious groups who would want to coerce my behavior in the direction of their religiously preferred standards."[10] I call this the

---

[10]Robert Audi, *Religion in the Public Square*, ed. Robert Audi and Nicholas Wolterstorff (Lanham, Md.: Rowman & Littlefield, 1997), p. 51.

golden-rule-contract argument, because (1) it seems to be modeled after Jesus' golden rule that we ought to do unto others as we want them to do unto us,[11] and (2) it seems to leave the justification of this rule to a social agreement or contract between disagreeing parties.

There are questions that one may raise about this argument. First, it is not clear what to make of the phrase "religiously preferred standards," since a standard, especially a religious one, is not the sort of thing that ought to be obeyed because those under its authority prefer, or choose, it. The Ten Commandments, for example, according to the Jewish and Christian traditions, ought to be obeyed, not because Jews and Christians religiously prefer the Decalogue, but rather, because its source is God and one ought to obey God even if one prefers to do otherwise. To refer to a religious standard as "preferred" assumes a consumer-model of religious belief that robs it of its status as a "standard." For preferences, like matters of taste, are not the types of beliefs that tell us what we ought to do. It is one thing to say I prefer that embryos not be experimented on, but it is quite another to say that embryos ought not be experimented on regardless of what you or I may prefer.

Second, Audi's argument is set at too high a level of abstraction. What does that mean? It means that Audi is making a claim that is not specific enough. It would be as if someone said, "Do good and love others." Although that is a correct precept, it cannot help us figure out what do in specific cases, such as whether it is good for the government to have a food stamps program or raise the speed limit from twenty-five to thirty-five. Consider this illustration. Suppose Fred, a white slave owner who embraces a religion that requires that its male members practice polygamy, does not agree with a religiously motivated abolitionist, Sam, who wants to criminalize slavery because he believes that black slaves, like their white owners, are made in the image of God and ought to be accorded all the rights that accompany such a status. Fred, relying on Audi's principle, explains to Sam: "How would you like it if I used the coercive power of the law to require that the male members of your sect practice polygamy, as is required by my faith? You would not like it, would you?

---

[11]"Do to others what you would have them do to you, for this sums up the Law and the Prophets" (Mt 7:12 NIV).

So, why don't you follow my example and show the kind of restraint to me that I have shown to you. Just as I should not force you to practice polygamy, you should not force me to abandon my ownership of slaves."

So just because the Christian would not like to be coerced by the state, does not mean he ought to restrain from coercing others. The fact is that Christians, like all citizens who believe they are correct in their political beliefs, think that their political views are true and that their community ought to embrace them for the sake of the common good. To tell Christians, or any collection of citizens, that they ought not to try to pass laws that may limit others' liberty because those others could do the same to them, suggests that citizens should be more concerned with their own interests than with the common good. But as Christians, we are told precisely the opposite: "Do nothing from selfish ambition or conceit, but in humility regard others as better than yourselves. Let each of you look not to your own interests, but to the interests of others" (Phil 2:3-4 NRSV). Or, as the late President John F. Kennedy (1917-1963) put it: "Ask not what your country can do for you—ask what you can do for your country."[12]

Third, Audi's argument assumes a "desire" account of self-interest. But this is a controversial understanding of liberty and the human person. It equates a person's good with the freedom to achieve what he or she desires in accordance with a chosen life plan. Although many people embrace this view, it is not obvious why we should assume the correctness of it, and Audi provides no arguments to defend it. After all, one can arrive at a completely different conclusion if one begins with what is called a *perfectionist view of liberty and the human person.*

What is perfectionism as applied to politics? It is the view that liberty is not merely the right to do good and that the role of government is to advance the common good. It is called *perfectionism* since its defenders maintain that human beings share the same nature by which we can know what sort of goods, institutions, habits and actions help the human being fulfill his proper end or perfection. For example, the end

---

[12]John F. Kennedy, "Inaugural Address" (January 20, 1961). Available at <www.jfklibrary.org/Historical+Resources/Archives/Reference+Desk/SpeechesJFK/003POF03Inaugural01201961.htm>.

(or purpose) of the mind is to know. Thus, ignorance is inconsistent with the mind's perfection. Consequently, it interferes with the common good when the state does not teach or direct its citizens to resist ignorance even if these citizens desire ignorance and believe it is in their self-interest to acquire it. Because desiring ignorance is wrong, and because no one has the right to do wrong, no real liberty is obstructed if the state impedes those who seek ignorance.

Because human beings are diverse in their abilities, talents and gifts, a free society with a perfectionist understanding would be one in which a full array of rights would be in place so that a wide variety of citizens would be able to lead flourishing lives and thus contribute to the common good. So, for example, freedom of expression, religious liberty, freedom of association, ownership of private property and personal privacy are liberties that are necessary so that citizens may be able to make informed judgments in light of their own talents, abilities, interests and beliefs.[13] However, these liberties are not ends in themselves. For instance, unless friendship and knowledge are goods, the freedoms of association and expression are pointless. Moreover, certain types of nonliberal associations—for example, families, churches, civic groups—play an important role in the moral and social formation of the nation's citizens. Families, for example, are nondemocratic institutions (i.e., children don't vote for their dad and mom) that provide a pride-of-place for the protection and moral formation of children, the sanctity of the marital bond, and a private community in which we all first learn how to treat and care for others. Thus, the perfectionist maintains, paradoxically, that liberal democracy functions best when nonliberal institutions are afforded certain liberties to flourish so that they may do their part in advancing the common good. Thus, the community has an interest in ensuring that these good and important culture-shaping institutions are not undermined by other practices. For this reason, in a perfectionist regime, the community may rightly exclude from social legitimacy many apparently private practices, such as polygamy, unregulated distribution and consumption of pornography, wife-swapping,

---

[13]For a perfectionist defense of these and other liberties, see Robert P. George in *Making Men Moral: Civil Liberties and Public Morality* (New York: Oxford University Press, 1993), chap. 5.

homosexual "marriage," child-marriage, honor killings, racist policies or consensual adult incest. The community may try to achieve its end in numerous ways, including total prohibition such as in the cases of honor killings and child marriage where severe and direct harm to innocent third parties takes place.

However, because the Christian perfectionist is committed to the Pauline precept, "if it be possible . . . live peaceably with all men" (Rom 12:18), he must be extremely careful that the policies he supports (when third-party harms are not at issue) are not draconian and that the tone in which he offers them is not disrespectful of the citizens with whom he disagrees. For this reason, Christians must make it clear to their fellow citizens that it is for the purpose of nurturing and protecting the common good and for the sake of the dignity of all persons, including those with whom they disagree, that they offer and support these policies.

In this regard, the great Christian philosopher Thomas Aquinas (1225-1274) points out that "human government," as Paul (Rom 13:1-7) and Peter (1 Pet 2:11-17) each claim, "is derived from the Divine government." For this reason, Thomas writes, the former should imitate the latter: "Now although God is all-powerful and supremely good, nevertheless He allows certain evils to take place in the universe, which He might prevent, lest, without them, greater goods might be forfeited, or greater evils ensue. Accordingly in human government also, those who are in authority, rightly tolerate certain evils, lest certain goods be lost, or certain greater evils be incurred: thus Augustine says (De Ordine ii, 4): 'If you do away with harlots, the world will be convulsed with lust.'"[14]

Although Thomas was a perfectionist, in the sense that he believed that a just political regime must be grounded on the principles of natural law, he saw human lawmaking as an activity of practical reason. It is in that sense Thomas was a *realist*. That is, when crafting human law, legislators must take into consideration the community to which the law is to be applied as well as the universal truth of the fallen nature of human beings. Writes Thomas:

---

[14]Thomas Aquinas *Summa Theologica* II-II, q. 10, art. 11, trans. Fathers of the English Dominican Province, 2nd rev. ed. (1920) <www.newadvent.org/summa/3010.htm>.

Now human law is framed for a number of human beings, the majority of whom are not perfect in virtue. Wherefore human laws do not forbid all vices, from which the virtuous abstain, but only the more grievous vices, from which it is possible for the majority to abstain; and chiefly those that are to the hurt of others, without the prohibition of which human society could not be maintained: thus human law prohibits murder, theft and such like. . . .

The purpose of human law is to lead men to virtue, not suddenly, but gradually. Wherefore it does not lay upon the multitude of imperfect men the burdens of those who are already virtuous, viz. that they should abstain from all evil. Otherwise these imperfect ones, being unable to bear such precepts, would break out into yet greater evils: thus it is written (Psalm 30:33): "He that violently bloweth his nose, bringeth out blood"; and (Matthew 9:17) that if "new wine," i.e. precepts of a perfect life, "is put into old bottles," i.e. into imperfect men, "the bottles break, and the wine runneth out," i.e. the precepts are despised, and those men, from contempt, break into evils worse still.[15]

Relying on Scripture and what it teaches about human nature, Thomas suggested that modesty and prudence should mark the character and judgments of the legislator. For this reason, the contemporary Christian should resist the temptation to cooperate with those, on either the right or the left, who promise that their policies will actualize a utopian vision of a just society. As we learned all too well from the bloody twentieth century, totalizing visions of the state and its powers never end well.

With this understanding of perfectionism in place, let us examine how the Christian perfectionist could apply Audi's principle and arrive at a different conclusion than Audi does. Recall his principle: "[It] is a kind of restraint I would wish to be observed by members of other religious groups who would want to coerce my behavior in the direction of their religiously preferred standards."[16] According to Audi, this means, for example, that a Christian prolifer should not try to pass laws that would prevent her neighbor from having an abortion, since the Chris-

---

[15]Ibid., I-II, q. 96, art. 2 <www.newadvent.org/summa/2096.htm>.
[16]Audi, *Religious Commitment*, p. 51.

tian prolifer would not like her neighbor's views forced on her.

Now we are ready to see how a Christian perfectionist, committed to a particular understanding of liberty and the human person, could assume his own view and nevertheless employ Audi's principle to the perfectionist's advantage. So let us imagine a prefectionist saying this:

> Because I know that I have a weakness of will, and a propensity to do what is wrong if there are no legal barriers to discourage me, I am grateful when the state forbids a bad activity, such as abortion, active euthanasia, or the consumption of pornography. It liberates me from the call of temptation. Virtue is easier to attain when there is encouragement by members of the wider community and that encouragement is reflected in the legal framework. Because I believe that the legal framework ought to make it difficult for me to treat others and myself in a degrading and immoral way, and I am grateful when it does, I owe it to my fellow citizens to help make it easier for them to live a virtuous life as well. In this way, I am obeying the golden rule, since I am loving my neighbor as myself.

For the Christian perfectionist, the bad coercion occurs when the law is employed to make it more difficult for her and others to live the good life. Thus, the Christian perfectionist expects his nonperfectionist peers to restrain themselves when they want to commend certain behaviors, for example, homosexual activities, use of pornography, or making accessible certain practices, such as abortion, euthanasia and embryonic stem-cell research. As John Finnis puts it, a Christian perfectionist's proposed legislation "may manifest, not contempt, but a sense of equal human worth of those people, whose conduct is outlawed precisely on the ground that it expresses a serious misconception of, and actually degrades, human worth and dignity, and thus degrades their own personal worth and dignity, along with that of others who may be induced to share in or emulate their degradation."[17] The Christian perfectionist's understanding of virtue is, of course, informed by a controversial religious worldview (even if he or she has nonreligious arguments for his or her viewpoint). But this is no less true of the nonperfectionist understanding of the good life assumed in Audi's ar-

---

[17]John Finnis, "Legal Enforcement of 'Duties to Oneself': Kant v. Neo-Kantians," *Columbia Law Review* 67 (1987): 437.

gument. Francis A. Canavan, for example, asks us to consider the case of the legal status of active euthanasia (or physician-assisted suicide):

> The person whose life is to be terminated by euthanasia wants to die. He therefore claims the right to end his life, or have it ended by a doctor, on the premise that the only value of life is a purely subjective one, and his life is no longer of value to him. The argument against letting him choose death—when all subsidiary and distracting arguments about fully informed consent have been settled—must involve the principle that human life is a value in itself, an objective human good, that the state exists to protect. Faced with this issue, the U.S. Supreme Court could not pretend to be neutral by finding euthanasia to be included in the constitutional right to privacy, thus making life and death objects of private choice. So to decide would be to come down on one side of the controversy, that side which holds that life has only subjective value.[18]

What Canavan is saying is that when the state puts in place a policy that allows a particular type of behavior—in this case, the right to kill oneself—that policy's permissibility depends on the state implicitly affirming something else about the state's citizens and their dignity, namely that the value of one's life is a matter of mere choice, not much different than one's treatment of commodities like microwaves and televisions. This is hardly a "neutral" point of view. Perhaps other examples will make this clearer.

Recall the case of Catholic Charities in Massachusetts we covered in chapter two. After the state's supreme judicial court ruled that the state must issue marriage licenses to same-sex couples,[19] Catholic Charities received an order from the state that its child adoption agency could no longer exclude same-sex couples as adoptee parents, in spite of the fact that the Catholic Church believes same-sex unions to be deeply disordered and sinful. Rather than compromise its moral theology, Catholic Charities stopped offering children up for adoption.[20] So even though same-sex marriage is often defended as a "liberty" for gay couples, its

---

[18]Francis A. Canavan, *The Pluralist Game: Pluralism, Liberalism, and the Moral Conscience* (Lanham, Md.: Rowman & Littlefield, 1995), pp. 74-75.

[19]*Goodridge v. Dept. of Public Health*, 440 Mass. 309 (2003).

[20]Maggie Gallagher, "Banned in Boston," *The Weekly Standard*, May 16, 2006 <www.weekly standard.com/Content/Public/Articles/000/000/012/191kgwgh.asp>.

implementation led in this case to obstructing the religious liberty of Catholic Charities.

Consider another example. Suppose[21] that you are a parent who lives in a community in which pornography is widely distributed and easily accessible to adults.[22] It can be found with ease on the Internet, cable television (with outlets found in every home) and on the shelves of nearly every convenience store, movie rental business and book retailer. In addition, talk radio stations, which specialize in vulgar conversation, occasionally have guests from the adult film industry. Your children's friends and their parents sometimes listen to these programs when they drive together to work and school. While at home you tell your teenage sons that regular consumption of pornography is harmful to their souls and will give them a distorted view of women, and that this may have a negative effect on their future marriages. Moreover, you point out that since pornography appeals to the desires rather than to the intellect, it is not something that one can indulge in freely for very long, for one can become a slave to one's base desires. So, you tell your boys, "Even though I am forbidding you access to pornography, I am in reality giving you more freedom, for this restriction of your conduct will make it less likely that you will become a slave to your desires."

You quickly realize, however, that because of your community's unwillingness to create and nurture a climate in which access to pornography is severely regulated, it is next to impossible for you to adequately fulfill your parental duty (not to mention your duty as a citizen concerned with the moral ecology of your community). Moreover, because your boys are aware of all this, they begin to resent your restrictions, for they feel deprived of what other boys in your community have an easy opportunity to enjoy. But you live in a nonperfectionist community, a community that defines liberty as freedom to do whatever one pleases as long as one does not interfere with another's liberty to do the same. And any restrictions on another's liberty based on a disputed view of

---

[21]This paragraph and the following four paragraphs, including the two from George, are adapted from pages 128-29 of my essay, "Is Statecraft Soulcraft? Faith, Politics, and Legal Neutrality," in *Bioengagement*, ed. Nigel Cameron, Scott Daniels and Barbara White (Grand Rapids: Eerdmans, 2000), pp. 113-31.

[22]This illustration was inspired by a similar one given in George, *Making Men Moral*, p. 27.

the good life (such as Christian morality) is a violation of liberal democracy. Of course, you believe that non-perfectionism is disputed as well and, based on the very same doctrine of state neutrality used against the legislating of your perspective, ought not to have a privileged position in your community's legal and social framework. For it seems to you quite plain that your liberty to bring up your children in the way you choose is being severely hampered by someone else's "community standards." As Robert P. George points out:

> People, notably including children, are formed not only in households, but in neighborhoods, and wider communities. Parents can prohibit a certain act, but their likelihood of success in enforcing the prohibition, and transmitting to their children a genuine grasp of the wrongness of the prohibited act, will be lessened to the extent that others more or less freely perform the act.
>
> Whatever authority parents have over their children, they lack the authority to deprive other people in the community, or other people's children, of the legal liberty to perform immoral acts; only public officials possess authority of that kind. If, however, public authorities fail to combat certain vices, the impact of widespread immorality on the community's moral environment is likely to make the task of parents to rightly forbid their own children from, say, indulging in pornography, extremely difficult.[23]

So from your perspective, your community's liberty to enjoy pornography, and your government's unwillingness to do anything about it, restricts you and your freedom. Thus, it seems that the golden-rule-contract argument is not helpful in resolving political disputes, since it achieves contrary results depending on what understanding of the human person (or liberty) is assumed in the disputant's premises. Consequently, it cannot serve as a basis for establishing secular liberalism.

The secular reason argument. Audi offers another principle that may be employed to support secular liberalism, the secular reason requirement: "[O]ne has a prima facie obligation not to advocate or support any law or public policy that restricts human conduct, unless one has,

---

[23]Ibid.

and is willing to offer, adequate secular reason for this advocacy or support (say for one's vote)."[24] In addition to assuming the controversial view of liberty already assessed above, this principle requires that a citizen's reasons be "secular." But "secular" is not a relevant property of a reason that is offered in support of the strength or soundness of the conclusion that its advocate is advancing. "True," "false," "plausible," "implausible," "good" and "bad" are adjectives that we apply to reasons when we assess the property relevant to its purpose as part of an argument. A property is a characteristic had by something. So, for example, one can say, "The dog is brown," which means that the dog has the property of "brownness." However, if one were to say, "The set of all even numbers is brown," one would be saying nonsense, since numerical sets cannot have the property of color. But reasons, like dogs and numerical sets, are things that can only have certain types of relevant properties. Just as a dog cannot have the property of "irrational number" and a numerical set cannot have the property of "blue," "loud" or "tall," a reason cannot be "secular." A reason does not gain more or less truth by being "secular." For "secular," like "tall," "fat," "stinky" or "sexy," has no bearing on the quality of the reason one may offer in an argument to advocate a particular public policy or point of view.

Consider this example. Suppose one believes the conclusion that unjust killing is morally wrong, and offers two reasons for it:

(1) The Bible forbids unjust killing.

(2) The philosopher Immanuel Kant's categorical imperative forbids unjust killing.

Most people would call (1) a religious reason and (2) a secular reason, since the first contains the name of a religious book, the Bible, and the second contains a nonreligious principle, the categorical imperative. But how do the terms *religious* and *secular* add to or subtract from our assessment of the quality of these reasons? If one has good reason to reject the authority of the Bible, then that good reason and not the religious nature of the Bible is the real reason why one ought to reject reason (1). On the other hand, suppose that one has good reasons to

---

[24]Audi, *Religion in the Public Square*, p. 25.

believe that the Bible is a better guide to moral philosophy than Kant's categorical imperative. In that case, one ought to conclude that (1) is a better reason than (2). But, again, how do the properties of "religious" and "secular" affect such a judgment? At the end of the day, a reason is weak or strong, true or false. Thus, "religious" and "secular" are not relevant properties when assessing the quality of reasons people may offer as part of their arguments.

In practice, this requirement for a secular reason functions as a hindrance to properly understanding the issues addressed, and the positions held, by many Christian citizens. Consider again the speech we assessed in chapter two. (I will repeat and expand on what I cover there.) Ron Reagan, the son of the late U.S. President Ronald W. Reagan, gave the speech at the 2004 Democratic National Convention.[25] Commenting on Americans who oppose embryonic stem-cell research, the younger Reagan argued:

> Now, there are those who would stand in the way of this remarkable future, who would deny the federal funding so crucial to basic research. They argue that interfering with the development of even the earliest stage embryo, even one that will never be implanted in a womb and will never develop into an actual fetus, is tantamount to murder. . . . [M]any are well-meaning and sincere. Their belief is just that, an article of faith, and they are entitled to it.
>
> But it does not follow that the theology of a few should be allowed to forestall the health and well-being of the many. And how can we affirm life if we abandon those whose own lives are so desperately at risk?[26]

Reagan then offers an account of the value of nascent life. He argues that early embryos "are not, in and of themselves, human beings,"[27] because they "have no fingers and toes, no brain or spinal cord. They have no thoughts, no fears. They feel no pain."[28] And because the early embryo's cells have yet to develop into the cells of specific organs or

---

[25]Ron Reagan, "Ron Reagan's Remarks at the Democratic Convention" (July 29, 2004). Transcript available at <www.usatoday.com/news/politicselections/nation/president/2004-07-29-reagan-speech-text_x.htm>.

[26]Ibid.

[27]Ibid.

[28]Ibid.

systems (i.e., they have not differentiated), and it is therefore just a cluster of "undifferentiated cells multiplying in a tissue culture" and not "a living, breathing person—parent, a spouse, a child,"[29] the embryo's stem cells may be used by researchers even if the extraction of those cells will result in the embryo's demise.

But by sequestering early embryos from the class of moral subjects, Ron Reagan attempts to answer a question of philosophical anthropology[30] that religious traditions also offer an answer. Reagan presents an argument in order to justify killing early embryos by trying first to answer the question of the nature of a moral subject. Those who oppose Reagan's position, mostly Christians, present arguments and counterarguments in order to first show that the early embryo is a moral subject and then, from there, show that killing that entity in the way that Reagan suggests is unjustified. Reagan chooses to call this position "an article of faith," even though its advocates offer real arguments with real conclusions and real reasons.[31] Of course, these arguments and the beliefs they support are, for many of their advocates, articles of faith, but they are also offered as deliverances of rational argument. In that case, they should be assessed on their merits as arguments.

Thomas Aquinas offered an understanding of faith and reason that may be helpful for understanding Ron Reagan's mistake, an error that is often made by secular (and some Christian) scholars in politics and law who are unfamiliar with the rigor and sophistication of Thomas's perspective.[32] For Thomas, there are things that can be known by rea-

---

[29]Ibid.

[30]As noted in chapter 2, "philosophical anthropology" deals with questions about the nature of human beings, such as what constitutes a human being, whether human beings have immaterial natures, souls, or minds and/or whether the absence or presence of those attributes or properties determines a human being's status as a moral subject.

[31]See, for example, Francis J. Beckwith, *Defending Life: A Moral and Legal Case Against Abortion Choice* (New York: Cambridge University Press, 2007); Francis J. Beckwith, "The Explanatory Power of the Substance View of Persons," *Christian Bioethics* 10, no. 1 (2004): 33-54; Patrick Lee, *Abortion and Unborn Human Life* (Washington, D.C.: Catholic University of America Press, 1996); Patrick Lee, "The Prolife Argument from Substantial Identity: A Defense," *Bioethics* 18, no. 3 (2004): 249-63; Patrick Lee and Robert P. George, "The Wrong of Abortion," in *Contemporary Debates in Applied Ethics*, ed. Andrew I. Cohen and Christopher Wellman (2005), pp. 13-26; J. P. Moreland and Scott B. Rae, *Body and Soul: Human Nature and the Crisis in Ethics* (Downers Grove, Ill.: InterVarsity Press, 2000).

[32]See Thomas Aquinas *Summa Theologica* I, q. 1 <www.newadvent.org/summa/1001.htm>.

son, things that can be known by faith, and things that can be known by both. For example, the periodic table in chemistry can be known by reason, the Trinity can be known only by special revelation (faith), and God's existence can be known by reason (philosophical arguments for God's existence) and faith (revelation), though things known by faith alone can never be contrary to reason. There is no two-tier view of knowledge for Thomas, for objects of faith are truly known and may count against someone's apparent deliverances of "reason," and it is the job of the philosopher to show that such deliverances are in fact against reason.

The difference between objects of faith and objects of reason for Thomas is not in their status as objects of knowledge, but in how the knowledge is acquired by the human mind. Take, for example, the case of the existence and nature of God. According to Thomas, one can know through reason that there is an eternally existing, necessary and personal agent that is the first cause of all that contingently exists. But that such a being is a Trinity—three persons and one eternal substance—is known as a consequence of philosophical reflection on the nature of the divinity revealed in special revelation, Scripture, and is not the result of the deliverances of reason alone. Still, in rebutting the charge that the Trinity is against reason, the philosopher may offer conceptual clarity to the skeptic and show that the doctrine is not incoherent or irrational. In that sense, the philosopher is showing that that which is known by faith (the Trinity) is not contrary to reason, even as he maintains that God's existence is known by both reason and faith, and thus is contrary to neither.[33]

It goes without saying, of course, that the political arguments offered by Christian citizens may not be as strong as their advocates think they are, that is, they may in fact be "against reason." But this may also be the case with the arguments presented by those, like Reagan, who hold contrary points of view. Consequently, calling the positions of Christian citizens "articles of faith" serves as a type of argument-stopper rather than advancing reasoned discourse. If, in fact, reason re-

---

[33]This paragraph and the prior one are adapted from portions of pages 54 and 55 of my review-essay, "What's Upstairs?" *First Things: A Monthly Journal of Religion and Public Life* 147 (November 2004): 51-52, 54-55 (reviewing Nancy Pearcey's *Total Truth*).

quires that we conclude that bioethical claims connected to theological traditions can never in principle be items of knowledge, then Reagan and his more sophisticated allies would have a point. But that case has yet to be made. And it seems that just the opposite is true, that religious believers seem well-prepared to rationally engage their secular opponents on a variety of subjects, including the rationality of religious belief itself as well as a variety of bioethical issues.[34] It seems, then, that there is little justification for believing that as long as we can convince our peers that a view is or may be "religious" we are relieved of our epistemic duty to rationally assess that view as a serious contender to the deliverances of so-called secular reason.

I must also briefly mention a legal variation on the secular reason requirement that I dealt with in chapter 3. Some thinkers have argued that the secular reason requirement can be justified by the religion clauses of the First Amendment, as well as by the philosophical principles that these thinkers believe gave rise to our contemporary understanding of these clauses. For example, Paul D. Simmons, in writing about the issue of abortion, suggests that the Supreme Court should "examine abortion as an issue of religious liberty and First Amendment guarantees."[35] According to Simmons, the position of abortion opponents—the fetus is a person from conception—is the result of "speculative metaphysics," indeed "religious reasoning," and for that reason, ought not to be part of public policy, because if it were it would amount to one religious position being foisted on those who do not agree with it. This would violate the establishment clause, the portion of the U.S. Constitution's First Amendment that asserts that government may not establish a religion.[36] It would also violate the free-exercise clause of the

---

[34]See the bioethical works cited in note 31 and Alvin Plantinga, *Warranted Christian Belief* (New York: Oxford University Press, 2000); Richard Swinburne, *The Existence of God* (New York: Oxford University Press, 1979); Alvin Plantinga and Nicholas Wolterstorff, eds., *Faith and Rationality: Reason and Belief in God* (Notre Dame, Ind.: University of Notre Dame Press, 1983); William Lane Craig, *The Kalam Cosmological Argument* (New York: Macmillan, 1979); Alvin Plantinga, *God and Other Minds: A Study of the Rational Justification of Belief in God* (Ithaca, N.Y.: Cornell University Press, 1967); Francis J. Beckwith, William Lane Craig and J. P. Moreland, eds., *To Everyone an Answer: A Case for the Christian Worldview* (Downers Grove, Ill.: InterVarsity Press, 2004).

[35]Simmons, "Religious Liberty and Abortion Policy," p. 88.

[36]Although the original purpose of the establishment clause of the First Amendment was to

First Amendment, for to allow such a public policy would be inconsistent with the Court's obligation "to protect the free exercise of the woman's conscientious (i.e., religious) judgment."[37]

But as we saw in our critique of Reagan, no matter what position the government takes on the nature of the embryo or fetus, it must rely, whether explicitly or implicitly, on some view of the human person tied to a metaphysical position that answers precisely the same sort of question that the "religious" positions to which Simmons alludes try to answer. Because these so-called "religious positions," as I have mentioned already, are often defended by arguments that are public in their quality and do not rely on crude appeals to holy Scripture or religious authority, it is not precisely clear why a public argument that is informed by a citizen's religious belief violates the Constitution while a contrary public argument that is informed by a citizen's secular belief does not.[38]

The err-on-the-side-of-liberty argument. Philosopher Judith Jarvis Thomson offers the most sophisticated version of Audi's secular reason requirement. Although she deals with the issue of abortion, one can easily extend her reasoning to other political issues, such as embryonic stem-cell research, cloning and physician-assisted suicide.

In this ingenious argument, Thomson concedes that the prolife position on abortion is not obviously irrational. (What she means by "not obviously irrational" is that if you are prolife, you are not crazy or stupid for believing that the unborn is a human person from conception. To say that it is rational, or not irrational, for one to believe something does not mean that one must believe it—like the belief that 2 + 2 = 4 or that the sun is a star. It just means that the case for the truth of the belief is plausible even though another person may remain unconvinced because the case against its truth is plausible as well.) Although Thomson concedes the religious roots of the prolife is position—for she calls

---

restrain *Congress* ("Congress shall make no law respecting an establishment of religion . . ."), the Supreme Court has incorporated the First Amendment through the Fourteenth Amendment and now applies the former to the states as well. See *Everson v. Board of Education* 330 U.S. 1 (1947).

[37]Simmons, "Religious Liberty and Abortion Policy," p. 88.

[38]For a more extensive critique of arguments by Simmons and others, see Beckwith, *Defending Life*, chap. 3.

one argument for it a Catholic argument[39]—she does not seem to think that the position's genesis is relevant to assessing the quality of the case offered for it. Thomson maintains that because she knows of no conclusive argument that would fatally count against the prolife position, the prolifer is not irrational in holding her views about the fetus's personhood and the moral wrongness of abortion that is entailed by it (and the legal implications of that judgment as well).

But this modest assessment of the rationality of prolife beliefs implies that the abortion-rights supporter is not rationally required to accept the prolife position. Conversely, reason does not require that the prolifer change her beliefs about the moral wrongness of abortion. Consequently, the prolifer's position is not so strong that a rational citizen may not reasonably disagree with this view and be within her rights in denying the fetus's personhood and thus be perfectly rational if she chooses to procure an abortion.[40] Thus, from a strictly rational point of view, no one side in this debate can legitimately claim to offer the position that reason requires. If this were a case in a criminal court, we would say that the evidence for the defendant's guilt is good but not beyond a reasonable doubt. Thus, both the prosecutor and the defense attorney are offering reasonable arguments that support their cases, but neither one has adequately refuted the arguments of the other. A jury in such a case would be required to deliver a verdict of not guilty.

Nevertheless, Thomson supports abortion's continued legalization. She does so, ironically, by employing to her advantage the dispute's impasse. She writes:

> One side says that the fetus has a right to life from the moment of conception, the other side denies this. Neither side is able to prove its case. . . . [W]hy should the deniers win? . . . The answer is that the situation is not symmetrical. What is in question here is not which of two values we should promote, the deniers' or the supporters'. What the supporters want is a license to impose force; what the deniers want is a license to be free of it. It is the former that needs justification.[41]

---

[39]Thomson, "Abortion."
[40]See, generally, ibid.
[41]Ibid.

The principle to which Thomson appeals to support this case is this: "severe constraints on liberty may not be imposed in the name of considerations that the constrained are not unreasonble in rejecting."[42] What she is saying is this: if the reason why you want to restrict my liberty is a reason that I can rationally reject, then you have no right to restrict my liberty. So, for example, if you try to restrict my liberty to carve pumpkins during Halloween because you believe that pumpkins are persons, and it is not irrational for me to think your belief is unconvincing, then you have no right to stop me from carving pumpkins. So unlike Audi, Thomson is not offering an argument that would exclude religiously informed cases for political positions. But rather, she is arguing that when there is deep disagreement over whether a particular act ought to be prohibited by the law, and the best arguments for those on all sides (including religiously informed arguments) are not obviously irrational, society ought to err on the side of liberty and permit the activity. After all, those who want to engage in the activity, abortion, are not irrational in rejecting the grounds for prohibiting it.

Thomson stipulates that liberty is the value at stake in the debate over abortion. But is she right about that? Consider first this example. Imagine there is a shooting range in Glendale, Arizona, that is situated 1,000 feet from an elementary school playground. At the request of concerned parents and citizens, the city council passes an ordinance that forbids operation of the shooting range while children are present on the playground during recess time. In its deliberations, which include expert witnesss testimony, the council finds that there is a 1 in 1,000 chance of a stray bullet striking a child on the playground during recess if the range is operating at full capacity during that time. Suppose that the local marksmen lobbying group, which believes its liberty is being unjustly obstructed by the ordinance, attempts to rebut this reasoning by offering Thomson's principle to the council: "Severe constraints on liberty may not be imposed in the name of considerations that the constrained are not unreasonable in rejecting." But this does not seem persuasive. The reason is that Thomson's principle does not

---

[42]Ibid.

provide us with any real guidance when one faction in a dispute is arguing that the exercise of the liberty in question results in a worse harm than the unjust constraint claimed by the other faction. To better grasp this problem, imagine the city council responds to the marksmen's application of Thomson's principle in the following way: "Yes, your principle may be correct, but the city is not unreasonable in constraining your liberty, for it is clearly not unreasonable that you acquiesce to a public policy that protects the innocent from unjust harm even if there is only a 1 in 1,000 chance of that harm occurring." The application of this reasoning to Thomson's argument should be obvious: Thomson's principle may be correct, but it would follow from it that one is not ureasonable in incorporating into law the prolife constraint on the pregnant woman's liberty, for Thomson's argument concedes that the prolife position on a fetus's personhood is reasonable and thus implicitly admits that most abortions may be cases of unjust homicide. After all, the burden that abortion is employed to terminate (pregnancy) is less of a harm than the wrong that Thomson concedes is not unreasonable for one to believe occurs in the termination of that burden, unjustifed homicide. Consequently, if it is reasonable for the city council to limit the liberty of marksmen because there is a chance of endangering moral subjects, then it is not unreasonable for prolifers to employ the resources of law to severely restrict the right to abortion.

Think about it.[43] If it is true, as Thomson claims, that no one position on the unborn's moral status wins the day, this is an excellent reason *not* to permit abortion, because an abortion *may* result in the death of a human entity who has a full right to life. If one kills another being without knowing whether that being is an entity with protected moral status, and if one has reasonable grounds (as Thomson admits) to believe that the being in question has that status, such an action would constitute a willful and reckless disregard for others, even if one later discovered that the being was not a person.

Thomson seems to be saying that the different positions on the fe-

---

[43]This paragraph and the three that follow are adapted from portions of my article, "Thomson's 'Equal Reasonableness' Argument for Abortion Rights: A Critique," *American Journal of Jurisprudence* 49, no. 1 (2004): 196-97.

tus's moral status all have able defenders, persuasive arguments and passionate advocates, but none really wins the day. To put it another way, the issue of fetal personhood is up for grabs; all positions are in some sense equal, none is better than any other. In fact, Thomson writes that "while I know of no conclusive reason for denying that fertilized eggs have a right to life, I also know of no conclusive reason for asserting that they do have a right to life."[44] But if this is the case, then it is safe to say that the odds of the fetus being a human person are 50/50. Given these odds, it would seem that society has a moral obligation to err on the side of life and, therefore, to legally prohibit virtually all abortions.

Imagine the police are able to identify someone as a murderer with only one piece of evidence: his DNA matches the DNA of the genetic material found on the victim. The police subsequently arrest him, and he is convicted and sentenced to death. Suppose, however, that it is discovered several months later that the murderer has an identical twin brother who was also at the scene of the crime and obviously has the same DNA as his brother on death row. This means that there is a 50/50 chance that the man on death row is the murderer. Would the state be justified in executing this man? Surely not, for there is a 50/50 chance of executing an innocent person. Consequently, if it is wrong to kill the man on death row, it is then wrong to kill the fetus when the arguments for its full humanity are just as reasonable as the arguments against it.

Although the preservation of liberty is certainly vital to sustaining a liberal democracy, the question of who is a proper subject of that liberty—whether or not it includes the unborn and the marginalized—is far more important. For if politics is about how the community ought to govern itself, then the question of who is a member of that community is the most important question of all.

CONCLUSION

Secular liberalism cannot remedy the deep philosophical conflicts that percolate beneath the political debates in which Christians have be-

---

[44]Thomson, "Abortion."

come vibrant participants. For its application results in what Canavan calls the pluralist game,[45] a bait and switch in which a religiously neutral public square that respects pluralism is promised so that our legal regime may avoid the imposition of any "sectarian" or "religious" dogma. But that is not what is delivered. What arrives is a legal regime that is no less sectarian than any of the "religious" views it was intended to sequester. As we have seen, secular liberalism presupposes and entails its own understandings of liberty and the human good that answer precisely the same philosophical questions that the so-called sectarian views answer.[46]

Consequently, contrary to some depictions of Christian involvement in politics, such religious citizens seem not to have inserted themselves into the public square because of a desire to "force their morality on others" (if we use the common pejorative description). Rather, they have become politically active for the purpose of resisting what they believe are understandings of the human person that are contrary to human dignity and thus the common good.

---

[45]See Canavan, *Pluralist Game*, pp. 63-80.
[46]See ibid., pp. 115-23.

5

GOD, NATURAL RIGHTS
AND THE NATURAL MORAL LAW

In chapter two we examined the idea of liberal democracy and the Christian's obligations as a citizen. We saw that a Christian may embrace this form of government without compromising her faith commitment. This does not mean, of course, that every act or policy of such a government is just or good. In such cases, the Christian citizen has an opportunity, within the strictures of such a government, to offer a remedy. And this is precisely why this form of government is fitting for a Christian. For it provides public space and protection for Christians (and others) to act for the advancement of justice. It does so within a cluster of overlapping institutions and governments with separated powers constrained by state and federal constitutions that include numerous protections, powers and judicial avenues of redress for their citizens. It may not be perfect, but it is constructed in such a way that it takes into account both humanity's propensity for evil (hence, the separation of powers of republican governments) as well as its dignity (hence, the notion of fundamental constitutional rights, representative governments and judicial bodies for the hope of redressing wrongs and establishing rights).

But the American Founders understood that the government they put in place presupposed a cluster of rights that citizens have by nature and that the government is obligated to recognize. They clearly spelled this out in the Declaration of Independence: "We hold these truths to be self-evident, that all men are created equal, that they are endowed by their Creator with certain unalienable Rights, that among these are Life, Liberty and the pursuit of Happiness."[1] Or, in the words of Alexander Hamilton, "the Sacred Rights of mankind are not to be rummaged for among old parchments or musty records. They are written, as with a sun beam, in the whole volume of human nature, by the Hand of the Divinity itself, and can never be erased or obscured by mortal power."[2]

But these rights imply a deeper understanding about the nature of human beings and the goods that are required for their flourishing. For example, if a human being possesses by nature a right to life, this means that other members of the community are morally obligated to not violate that right to life. But this seems to imply something about human beings and their nature that is moral in quality, a sacredness that requires us to treat each other with a certain dignity and respect. Thus, natural rights seem to imply a natural moral law.

Almost all citizens today seem to believe that there are natural rights that depend on a natural moral law, rights that the state is obligated to honor. For we believe that even if a legitimate legislative body passes a statute in accordance with the law, the statute still may be in violation of the natural moral law. So, for example, if slavery were to be reinstituted, our judgment of the law's wrongness would depend on a prior understanding of what it means to be a human being and why human beings are not, by nature, property. We would say that when someone is enslaved his rights are violated, even if the government under which this occurred did not recognize such rights. Moreover, the rights found in the U.S. Constitution's Bill of Rights seem to be based on the understanding that the good of human flourishing depends on human beings having certain freedoms or liberties.[3] Thus, as I noted in chapter four in our discussion of perfectionism, freedom of expression, religious liberty, freedom of association, ownership of private property and personal privacy are liberties that are necessary so that citizens may be able to make informed judgments in light of their own talents, abilities, in-

---

[1]U.S. Declaration of Independence (1776), par. 2.

[2]Alexander Hamilton, "The Farmer Refuted" (February 23, 1775). Available at <http://press-pubs.uchicago.edu/founders/documents/v1ch3s5.html>.

[3]See, for example, Paul R. DeHart, *Uncovering the Constitution's Moral Design* (Columbia: University of Missouri Press, 2007).

terests and beliefs.[4] However, these liberties are not ends in themselves. For instance, unless friendship and knowledge are goods, the freedoms of association and expression are pointless. Thus the natural rights affirmed in the Declaration of Independence and implied in the U.S. Constitution depend on the reality of certain fundamental goods, a natural moral law.

There are, of course, many complicated and important issues concerning the relationship between natural rights and natural law, such as the differences between the natural rights embraced by Thomas Hobbes (1588-1679) and John Locke and the natural law defended by Thomas Aquinas,[5] as well as the disputes between the new and traditional natural-law theorists.[6] In fact, some natural lawyers have suggested that we ought to chuck the idea of natural rights altogether because they come out of the Enlightenment,[7] which artificially and fatally separated reason from developed moral traditions. Although these and other issues are certainly worthy of serious assessment, in this chapter I will set them aside and focus on the more modest question of whether it is reasonable to believe that the natural moral law requires the existence of God, as the American Founders believed.

What I mean by *reasonable* is not that reason requires that one *must* believe it. Rather, what I am suggesting is something less ambitious, namely, that a citizen who believes that natural rights and natural law require the existence of God embraces a philosophically defensible position that he or she may legitimately claim is an item of knowledge. Nonbelieving citizens who disagree, therefore, are not irrational for doing so.

So in this chapter I address the question of whether it is reasonable to believe that the natural moral law requires the existence of God, as

---

[4]For a perfectionist defense of these and other liberties, see Robert P. George, *Making Men Moral: Civil Liberties and Public Morality* (New York: Oxford University Press, 1993), chap. 5.

[5]See J. Budziszewski, *Written on the Heart: The Case for Natural Law* (Downers Grove, Ill.: InterVarsity Press, 1997).

[6]See Michael Cromartie, ed., *A Preserving Grace: Protestants, Catholics, and Natural Law* (Grand Rapids: Eerdmans, 1997).

[7]"[T]here are no such rights, and belief in them is one with belief in witches and in unicorns" (Alasdair MacIntyre, *After Virtue: A Study in Moral Theory*, 2nd ed. [Notre Dame, Ind.: University of Notre Dame Press, 1984], p. 69).

the American Founders believed. In order to accomplish this, I first discuss how some contemporary atheists seem to presupppose a natural moral law. I then deal specifically with the question of whether the natural moral law suggests God. I conclude with a brief discussion on whether the idea of a natural moral law is biblical.

NATURAL MORAL LAW AND THE TESTIMONY OF CONTEMPORARY ATHEISM

Belief in a natural moral law is so widely held that it is rare to find anyone who does not believe in it. For example, the atheist Christopher Hitchens, in his book *God Is Not Great*, argues that "religion poisons everything," blaming religious believers and their beliefs for many of the atrocities of history.[8] Setting aside the question of Hitchens's historical accuracy and philosophical acumen,[9] his thesis assumes that human beings have had their rights violated by other human beings who committed their wicked deeds in the name of God and for bad reasons. Some of the cases that Hitchens cites do involve legitimate governments perpetuating and protecting wicked acts that they had the legal power to perpetuate and protect. And yet, this fact would not move Hitchens to say that the acts he thinks are wrong are now right. Why? Because human beings have certain rights by nature that the government is morally obligated to recognize and protect. In fact, Hitchens writes that he and other atheists "believe with certainty that an ethical life can be lived without religion,"[10] thus implying that he and others have direct and incorrigible acquaintance with a natural moral law that informs their judgments about what counts as an ethical life. Thus, the free-thinking posture that one finds on the prior page in Hitchens' book—"[W]hat we respect is free inquiry, openmindedness"[11]— becomes a stingy dogma a page later when it comes to the "ethical life."

---

[8]Christopher Hitchens, *God Is Not Great: How Religion Poisons Everything* (New York: Warner Books, 2007).

[9]A nice antidote to Hitchens's bizarre take on the influence of Christianity on history are the following works: Robert Royal, *The God That Did Not Fail* (San Francisco: Encounter Books, 2006); Rodney Stark, *For the Glory of God* (Princeton, N.J.: Princeton University Press, 2002); and Rodney Stark, *The Victory of Reason* (New York: Random House, 2005).

[10]Hitchens, *God Is Not Great*, p. 6.

[11]Ibid., p. 5.

But this is good, since no one would want Hitchens or any other person to begin to question the rationality of his moral opposition to rape, murder and theft.

Richard Dawkins, another prominent atheist, does something similar in his book *The God Delusion* when he laments the career path of Kurt Wise. According to Dawkins, Wise was at one time a promising young scholar who had earned a degree in geology (from the University of Chicago) and advanced degrees in geology and paleontology from Harvard University, where he studied under the highly acclaimed Stephen Jay Gould.[12] Wise is also a young-earth creationist, which means that he accepts a literal interpretation of the first chapters of Genesis, and maintains that the Earth is less than 10,000 years old. It is not a position I hold, and for that reason I am sympathetic to Dawkins's bewilderment of why Wise has embraced what appears to many Christians as a false choice between one controversial interpretation of Scripture (young-earth creationism) and abandoning Christianity altogether. (But that is another topic for another book.)

In any event, at one point in his career Wise began to understand that his reading of Scripture was inconsistent with the dominant scientific understanding of the age of the Earth and the cosmos. Instead of abandoning his reading of Scripture, he continued to embrace it, but this led to a crisis of faith. Wise writes: "Either the Scripture was true and evolution was wrong or evolution was true and I must toss out the Bible. . . . It was there that night that I accepted the Word of God and rejected all that would ever counter it, including evolution. With that, in great sorrow, I tossed into the fire all my dreams and hopes in science."[13] So Wise abandoned the possibility of securing a professorship at a prestigious research university or institute.

Dawkins is disturbed by Wise's theological judgment and its consequence on his obvious promise as a scholar, researcher and teacher. Writes Dawkins: "I find that terribly sad. . . . [T]he Kurt Wise story is

---

[12]Richard Dawkins, *The God Delusion* (London: Bantam, 2007), p. 284.
[13]Ibid., p. 285. According to Dawkins, this quotation from Wise is from an essay he contributed to the anthology, *In Six Days: Why 50 Believe in Creation*, ed. J. E. Ashton (Sydney: New Holland, 1999).

just plain pathetic—pathetic and contemptible. The wound, to his career and his life's happiness, was self-inflicted, so unnecessary, so easy to escape. . . . I am hostile to religion because of what it did to Kurt Wise. And if it did that to a Harvard educated geologist, just think what it can do to others less gifted and less well armed."[14]

Of course, some Christians may be just as troubled as Dawkins. One need not be an atheist to raise legitimate questions about Professor Wise's intellectual and spiritual journey. But, given Dawkins's atheism, there is something odd about his lament. It seems to require that Dawkins accept something about the nature of human beings and the natural moral law that his atheism seems to reject. Let me explain what I mean. Dawkins harshly criticizes Wise for embracing a religious belief that results in Wise not treating himself and his talents, intelligence and abilities in a way appropriate for their full flourishing. That is, given the opportunity to hone and nurture certain gifts—for example, intellectual skill—no one, including Wise, should waste them as a result of accepting a false belief. The person who violates, or helps violate, this norm, according to Dawkins, should be condemned and we should all bemoan this tragic moral neglect. But Dawkins's judgment of Wise makes sense only in light of Wise's particular talents and the sort of being Wise is by nature, a being that Dawkins seems to believe possesses certain intrinsic capacities and purposes that results in an injustice if prematurely disrupted. So the human being who wastes his talents is one who does not respect his natural gifts or the basic capacities whose maturation and proper employment make possible the flourishing of many goods. That is, the notion of "proper function,"[15] coupled with the observation that certain perfections grounded in basic capacities have been impermissibly obstructed from maturing, is assumed in the very judgment Dawkins makes about Wise and the way by which Wise should treat himself.

But Dawkins, in fact, does not actually believe that living beings, including human beings, have intrinsic purposes or are designed to al-

---

[14]Dawkins, *God Delusion*, pp. 285-86.
[15]See Alvin Plantinga, *Warrant and Proper Function* (New York: Oxford University Press, 1993).

low the conclusion that violating one's proper function amounts to a violation of one's moral duty to oneself. Dawkins has maintained for decades that the natural world only appears to be designed,[16] which means that his lament for Wise is misguided. For Dawkins is lamenting what only appears to be Wise's dereliction of his duty to nurture and employ his gifts in ways that result in his happiness and an acquisition of knowledge that contributes to the common good. But because there are no designed natures and no intrinsic purposes, and thus no natural duties that we are obligated to obey, the intuitions that inform Dawkins's judgment of Wise are as illusory as the design he explicitly rejects. But that is precisely one of the grounds on which Dawkins suggests that theists are irrational and ought to abandon their belief in God.[17] So if the theist is irrational for believing in God based on what turns out to be pseudodesign, Dawkins is irrational in his judgment of Wise and other creationists he targets for reprimand and correction. For Dawkins's judgment rests on a premise that he has uncompromisingly maintained throughout his career that only appears to be true. (Even if one finds Dawkins's views flawed, as I do, one need not embrace the arguments of the advocates of what has become known as intelligent design [ID] in order to rationally embrace intrinsic purpose or even design.)[18]

Thus the Christian agrees with Hitchens that human beings have rights by nature, and the Christian also agrees with Dawkins that human beings have an intrinsic purpose, or design, that places on each of us a moral obligation to nurture our natural gifts and abilities in a way

---

[16]Writes Dawkins: "Darwin and his successors have shown how living creatures, with their spectacular statistical improbability and appearance of design, have evolved by slow, gradual degrees from simple beginnings. We can now safely say that the illusion of design in living creatures is just that—an illusion" (Dawkins, *God Delusion*, p. 158).

[17]See ibid., chap. 3.

[18] See, for example, Francis J. Beckwith, "How to Be an Anti-Intelligent Design Advocate," *University of St. Thomas Journal of Law and Public Policy* 4, no. 1 (2009-2010); Edward Feser, *The Last Superstition: A Refutation of the New Atheism* (South Bend, Ind.: St Augustine's Press, 2008); Thomas W. Tkacz, "Thomas Aquinas vs. the Intelligent Designers: What Is God's Finger Doing in My Pre-Biotic Soup?" in *Intelligent Design: Real Science or Religion in Disguise?* ed. Robert Baird and Stuart Rosenbaum (Amherst, N.Y.: Prometheus, 2007), pp. 275-82; and Leon Kass, "The Permanent Limits of Biology," in *Life, Liberty and the Defense of Dignity: The Challenge for Bioethics* by Leon Kass (San Francisco: Encounter Books, 2002). Reprinted with permission at <www.catholiceducation.org/articles/medical_ethics/me0052.html>.

that helps them to come to fruition and achieve their natural end for the good of ourselves and our communities. So the Christian and these atheists agree on the existence of natural rights, a natural moral law and natural moral obligations, and that human beings have an intrinsic end or purpose that they may negligently or purposely fail to accomplish and be rightly judged immoral for such a failure.

Why the Natural Moral Law Suggests God

Because liberal democracy assumes natural rights, and because natural rights require a natural moral law, therefore, liberal democracy assumes a natural moral law. This, as we have seen, was the view of the signers of the Declaration of Independence, even though they disagreed on a variety of religious questions, including the truth of Christianity. Again, as we have seen, it seems that today both believers and unbelievers have these same intuitions.

Given this natural moral law, I now want to argue that the existence of God best accounts for these correct intuitions. The case I make is not a knock-down, drag-out proof for God's existence from the existence of a natural moral law. But rather, the case I make is much like a legal argument for a defendant's guilt in a criminal case. It is, in a sense, arguing that given the "fingerprints" that one finds on natural rights when one reflects on their nature, it seems that they are best explained as the result of the hand and mind of the God of theism. Although one may reject this conclusion, it is difficult to conceive of a better alternative. In the words of philosopher Paul Copan, "objective moral values [the basis of natural rights] are quite at home in a theistic universe. Given God's existence, moral realism is natural. But given an atheistic universe, . . . objective morality—along with its assumptions of human dignity, rights, and moral responsibility—is unnatural and surprising and 'queer.'"[19] Thus, there are really only two options for the origin of the natural moral law: (A) it exists, but it is an accident, a product of chance; and (B) it is the result of intelligence.

Option one: The natural moral law is a product of chance. If the natu-

---

[19]Paul Copan, "Can Michael Martin Be a Moral Realist? *Sic et Non*," *Philosophia Christi* 1 (1999): 58.

ral moral law is a product of chance, then it is a collection of brute facts that are the result of unguided, naturalistic evolution. (I say unguided and naturalistic evolution to distinguish it from theistic evolution, which affirms an evolutionary account of living organisms that is ultimately guided by God. A theistic evolutionist may, of course, consistently maintain that the moral law comes from God, which is why this critique only applies to atheistic evolutionists.)[20] But this does not seem adequate. For if moral norms have no mind behind them, then there is no justification to obey them. Consider this illustration: if while playing Scrabble, the letters randomly spell "Go to Baltimore," should I obey the command, buy a plane ticket, make hotel reservations and/or take up temporary residence in Baltimore? Of course not, for "the command" is a chance-created phrase and is really no command at all. As Gregory P. Koukl points out, "Commands are communications between two minds. Chance might conceivably create the appearance of a moral rule, but there can be no command if no one is speaking." A command created by accident "can be safely ignored."[21]

Suppose, however, that the evolutionary naturalist replies that morality exists because it is necessary for survival. According to this view, moral rules against adultery, murder, stealing, etc., are the result of the forces of natural selection "choosing" those genes that perpetuate traits that are more conducive to the preservation of the human species. In the words of Robert Wright: "If within a species there is variation among individuals in their hereditary traits, and some traits are more conducive to survival and reproduction than others, then those traits will (obviously) become more widespread within the population. The result (obviously) is that the species' aggregate pool of hereditary traits changes."[22] Behavioral patterns that help sustain

---

[20]See, for example, the work of the Christian theistic evolutionist, Francis S. Collins, appointed in 2009 by President Barack Obama as the director of the National Institutes of Health: *The Language of God: A Scientist Presents Evidence for Belief* (New York: The Free Press, 2006). He served from 1993 through 2008 as director of the National Human Genome Research Institute.

[21]Gregory P. Koukl in Francis J. Beckwith and Gregory P. Koukl, *Relativism: Feet Firmly Planted in Mid-Air* (Grand Rapids: Baker, 1998), p. 167.

[22]Robert Wright, *The Moral Animal: Evolutionary Psychology and Everyday Life* (New York: Pantheon, 1994): p. 23.

these species-preserving traits are part of what we call "morality."

So according to the evolutionary naturalist's understanding, a "Mind" is not a necessary condition to account for the diversity of natures of the living beings that arise out the vast eons during which natural selection cooperates with random genetic mutations and perhaps other evolutionary forces. But this human nature tells us nothing normative. It merely describes what is statistically ordinary and generally species-preserving. The evolutionary naturalist thinks that is all that we need to ground natural law.

According to Larry Arnhart, who calls himself a "Darwinian conservative,"[23] scholarship in political theory has incorporated this evolutionary understanding in order to account for the human sentiments that are the foundation of family life. Citing the work of renowned political scientist, James Q. Wilson, Arnhart writes:

> Wilson . . . argues that natural selection may have promoted a generalized psychological propensity to "attachment" or "affiliation." What he calls "affiliation" corresponds to what Aristotle calls "friendship" (philia): a natural drive to social bonding diversely expressed as sexual, familial, companionate, political, or philanthropic attachments. . . . Wilson believes the human sentiments of sympathy and benevolence, which throughout most of human evolutionary history would have enhanced reproductive fitness by inclining human parents to care for their young, can now be extended to people who are not offspring or even to nonhuman animals.[24]

There are, however, several problems with the evolutionary naturalist account. First, because helping the weak, the genetically marred and the social parasite is not evolutionarily helpful, why do we have a sense of duty to help those less fortunate than ourselves? Suppose the evolutionary naturalist answers that we would not have this sense of duty unless it were evolutionarily helpful. There are at least two problems with this answer. (1) It begs the question, for it assumes that whatever moral senses we have must be the result of unguided evolution. (Beg-

---

[23]Larry Arnhart, *Darwinian Conservatism* (Charlottesville, Va.: Imprint Academic, 2005).
[24]Larry Arnhart, "The New Darwinian Naturalism in Political Theory," *Zygon* 33, no. 3 (September 1998): 377 (citations omitted).

ging the question is a fallacy that occurs when one assumes what one is trying to prove, e.g., "The Lakers are the best team because no team is better.") But because the question is whether naturalistic evolution can explain all our moral senses, it is circular reasoning to assume that whatever moral senses we have must be the result of naturalistic evolution. (2) Because it is clear that not every human being has a moral sense that he or she has a duty to help those less fortunate than themselves, on what grounds could the evolutionary naturalist say that these human beings are mistaken in their moral viewpoint? After all, people who lack this moral sense have existed all over the globe for generations, and if they too are the products of unguided evolution, perhaps having such people in our population is necessary for the preservation of the species. If that is the case, then "moral sense" can only be judged on a person-by-person basis; it is not universally binding. But that undermines the notion of a natural moral law that atheists, such as Hitchens and Dawkins, must sustain in order to issue their strong, universal moral judgments against atrocities and wrongdoings committed throughout human history and across cultures in the name of religion. On the other hand, if the evolutionary naturalist bites the bullet and maintains that those who lack the moral sense to see that they have an obligation to those weaker than themselves are morally wrong, regardless of what moral sense they may feel, then there is a morality above naturalistic evolution by which we can make moral judgments about the moral senses of different segments of our population that resulted from unguided evolution. Thus naturalistic evolution lacks explanatory power in accounting for the natural moral law.

Second, naturalistic evolution is concerned only with the sorts of behavior that are conducive to the preservation of the species. But morality encompasses more than just behavior, including, among other things, motive and intent. In fact, a moral judgment is incomplete without taking these into consideration. For one can be immoral without any behavior, simply on the basis of motive and intent. For example, I can intend to carry out a murder and never do it. One can be immoral simply on the basis of motive and intent even if the behavior has "good" results. For example, if I intend to harm someone by tripping him, but end up preventing him from being hit by a car and thus save his life, the results are good even though what I did was immoral. "Bad" results may be part of a morally good act simply on the basis of motive and intent. For example, if a surgeon operates on a terminal patient with the intent to remove a cancer, but during the operation the patient dies of cardiac arrest, the surgeon has not acted immorally. Since naturalistic evolution, at best, can only describe what behaviors are conducive to the preservation of the species and does not address the role of motive and intent in evaluating those behaviors, naturalistic evolution is an inadequate explanation for the existence of the natural moral law.

Third, the naturalistic evolutionary explanation of morality is merely descriptive. That is to say, it merely tells us what behaviors in the past may have been conducive to the survival of the species and why I may, on occasion, have moral feelings to act consistently with those behaviors. But naturalistic evolution cannot tell me whether I ought to act on those feelings in the present and in the future. Granted, I am grateful that people in the past behaved in ways that made my existence possible. But why should I emulate only those behaviors that many people today say are "good"? After all, some people in the past raped, stole and murdered. And I know of many people today who have feelings to rape, steal and murder. Perhaps these behaviors are just as important for my existence and the preservation of the species as the "good" behaviors. Unless there is a morality above the morality of naturalistic evolution, it is difficult to see how one can distinguish between morally good and bad actions if both types may have been conducive to the preservation of the species.

Consequently, evolutionary naturalism may very well explain why each of us may have certain moral feelings on occasion. But it cannot say why citizen X ought to perform (or not perform) act Y in circumstance Z. To cite another example: Arnhart argues that the traditional family best protects and preserves the human species if it is widely practiced.[25] But what do we say to the eighty-something Hugh Hefner, who would rather shack up with five twenty-something buxom blondes

---

[25]Arnhart, *Darwinian Conservatism*, chap. 3.

with which he engages in carnal delights with the assistance of state-of-the-art pharmaceuticals? Mr. Hefner is no doubt grateful that his ancestors engaged in practices (e.g., the traditional family) that made his existence and lifestyle possible. But why should he emulate only those practices that many people today (e.g., Arnhart and I) say are "good"? After all, some of our ancestors were Hefnerian in their sensibilities, taking on a concubine or two and running off with one of them every once in a while. Perhaps this practice was just as necessary for Mr. Hefner's existence and the preservation of the species as were the "good" behaviors practiced by history's squares. Because we have always had in our population Hugh Hefners of one sort or another, it is not clear to me how Arnhart can distinguish between good and bad practices if both sorts may have played a part in the survival of the human race, unless there is a morality by which we assess the morality of unguided evolution. But this would seem to lead us back to a natural law that has its source in Mind and that is not subject to the unstable flux of naturalistic evolution.

Fourth, although the evolutionary naturalist seems to be correct that certain sentiments (e.g., love of family and children) are consistent with a natural law understanding of community, these sentiments themselves seem inadequate to ground moral action or to account for certain wrongs. For example, Tony Soprano's[26] love of kin nurtures sentiments that lead to clear injustices, for example, rubbing out enemies, about which Tony and family do not seem particularly troubled. In that case, the wrongness of the act is located not in the sentiments of its perpetrators (or even its victims, if the victims, for some reason, were convinced that they deserved to be rubbed out) but in a judgment informed by moral norms that stand above, and are employed by free agents, to assess acts and actors apart from their sentiments. Again, we are back to the natural law that has its source outside of naturalism's unguided torrent.

Option two: The natural moral law is the result of Mind. Because the natural moral law does not seem to be the product of chance, only one

---

[26]Tony Soprano is a fictional character in the HBO series *The Sopranos,* which ran from 1999-2007. In the show, Mr. Soprano (played by actor James Gandolfini) was the head of an organized mob family with its headquarters in New Jersey.

option remains: it has its source in an intelligence. What sort of intelligence could this being be? It must be the sort of being who could be the ground of a natural moral law. So it could not be a contingent intelligence, one whose existence and moral authority is dependent on something else outside itself. For in order to be the ground of morality, a being must not receive its existence and moral authority from another, for that other being, if it is not contingent, would then be the ground of the natural moral law. Therefore, the source of the moral law must be a self-existent, perfectly good being who has the juridical authority that requires that we owe him our duty to obey. It seems only fitting to call such a being "God." As Richard Taylor puts it, "A duty is something that is owed . . . but something can be owed only to some person or persons. There can be no such thing as a duty in isolation. . . . The concept of a moral obligation [is] unintelligible apart from the idea of God. The words remain, but the meaning is gone."[27]

Is the Natural Moral Law Biblical?

Although there are many Protestant defenders of the natural moral law,[28] there are some Protestant Christians who believe that it is "unbiblical," and thus un-Christian, to claim that one can know the natural moral law apart from special revelation, the Bible. They offer many arguments, though I will only briefly respond to two here.[29]

The Scripture argument. The first argument is that it is not possible to know the moral law apart from Scripture and the doctrines derived from it.[30] This is a weak argument, since Scripture itself teaches and in

---

[27]Richard Taylor, *Ethics, Faith and Reason* (Englewood Cliffs, N.J.: Prentice-Hall, 1985), pp. 83-84, as quoted in Beckwith and Koukl, *Relativism*, p. 168.

[28]See, for example, C. S. Lewis, *The Abolition of Man* (London: Oxford University Press, 1943); Norman L. Geisler, *Thomas Aquinas: An Evangelical Assessment* (Grand Rapids: Baker, 1991), pp. 163-75; J. Daryl Charles, "Protestants and Natural Law," *First Things* 168 (December 2006): 33-38; Michael Bauman, *Pilgrim Theology: Taking the Path of Theological Discovery* (Grand Rapids: Zondervan, 1992), pp. 203-8; and Beckwith and Koukl, *Relativism*.

[29]This section is adapted from portions of pages 36-38 of my article, "Doing What Comes Naturally and Not Knowing It: A Reflection on J. Budziszewski's Work," *The Catholic Social Science Review* 12 (2007): 33-40.

[30]See, for example, Alister E. McGrath, "Doctrine and Ethics," *Journal of the Evangelical Theological Society* 34, no. 2 (June 1991): 145-56.

many cases assumes the truth of the natural law.[31] Two examples will suffice, though there are many others I could offer.

As I noted in chapter two, the first crime recorded in the Bible is Cain's murder of Abel (Gen 4:1-16), even though there was at the time no written law (or Bible) to speak of. This means that one can know justice and injustice apart from governments or written law, that knowledge of the moral law does not depend on acquaintance with Scripture or any external earthly authority. For it is by the moral law that we judge governments and written laws as either just or unjust. That is why God could legitimately hold Cain accountable for his crime even though there were no criminal statutes or Scripture at the time.

The book of 2 Samuel (chap. 11) relates the story of King David's encounter with Nathan after the king had taken himself a wife, Bathsheba, a woman he had first encountered one evening while he strolled on the palace roof. He noticed, from a distance, Bathsheba bathing. Overwhelmed by her beauty, he sent his messengers to fetch her, and he quickly came to know her (in the biblical sense). That union, however, resulted in a pregnancy. This posed a problem since Bathsheba, as David knew, was married to Uriah the Hittite. So the king assigned Uriah, a member of the army, to the front lines where the fighting would be the most ferocious, and instructed Joab, the leader of the Israelite army, to leave Uriah there unprotected so that he would surely be killed. David married Bathsheba soon after Uriah died on the battlefield.

But David did not live happily ever after. First among the many punishments that followed for David came Nathan's rebuke, which Nathan introduced with an elegant form of moral reasoning that forced the king to confront the gravity of his offense:

> When [Nathan] came to [David], he said, "There were two men in a certain town, one rich and the other poor. The rich man had a very large number of sheep and cattle, but the poor man had nothing except one little ewe lamb he had bought. He raised it, and it grew up with him and

---

[31]See, for example, David VanDrunen, *A Biblical Case for Natural Law* (Grand Rapids: The Acton Institute, 2006); Alan F. Johnson, "Is There Biblical Warrant for Natural Law Theory?" *Journal of the Evangelical Theological Society* 25, no. 2 (June 1982): 185-99.

his children. It shared his food, drank from his cup and even slept in his arms. It was like a daughter to him.

"Now a traveler came to the rich man, but the rich man refrained from taking one of his own sheep or cattle to prepare a meal for the traveler who had come to him. Instead, he took the ewe lamb that belonged to the poor man and prepared it for the one who had come to him."

David burned with anger against the man and said to Nathan, "As surely as the LORD lives, the man who did this deserves to die! He must pay for that lamb four times over, because he did such a thing and had no pity."

Then Nathan said to David, "You are the man!" (2 Sam 12:1-7 NIV)

David fully grasped the moral principles by which we judge that the rich man's behavior as wicked and he also understood that such a breach should result in severe punishment against the rich man. But those very same moral principles and the punishments that follow from violating them applied to David as well. As should be obvious, Nathan was not appealing to the Bible, since there was no Bible as we know it today. What one takes away from this story is the wisdom of Nathan's judgment, the aptness of his analogy, and the clarity that one acquires when grasping a scintillating instance of moral reasoning. This is natural law reasoning at its best. And it is biblical.

Romans 1 and 2 do not teach about the natural moral law. The second argument goes like this: the scriptural passages most often cited in defense of natural law (e.g., Rom 1–2, especially Rom 2:15, which speaks of the law "written on our hearts") do not teach what natural law proponents think it teaches, namely, that there are moral truths accessible to those with no direct contact with special revelation. For example, evangelical theologian Carl F. H. Henry writes:

> The dual reference to law of nature and law of God presumably arose from the apostle Paul's teaching in Romans 1 and 2. John Murray in his volume on Paul's epistle to the Romans in The New International Commentary series argues that the term "law of nature" is a Christian concept rooted in Scripture, not a secular concept to be grasped independently of a revelatory epistemology. To interpret Romans 1 and 2 in deistic terms of natural religion is unjustifiable.[32]

---

[32]Carl F. H. Henry, "Natural Law and a Nihilistic Culture," *First Things* 49 (January 1995): 58.

Although this is not the place to assess Henry's exegesis, it seems to me that his scriptural citation is not based on a careful reading or understanding of natural law. Had he truly grasped the tradition he critiques, he would understand that his own point of view—the alleged biblical rejection of natural law theory—is itself dependent on moral notions not derived from special revelation. That is, Henry is affirming and defending a self-refuting position. Let me explain. By claiming that natural law thinkers have incorrectly interpreted the book of Romans, Henry is presupposing a moral notion that is logically prior to his exegesis of Scripture: texts should be interpreted accurately. This, of course, is grounded in more primitive moral notions: to accurately interpret a text one should do so fairly and honestly, and one should pursue the truth while interpreting texts. Both these moral commands are logically prior to, and thus not derived from, Scripture itself, for in order to extract truth from Scripture, obedience to these moral commands is a necessary condition. This means that Henry, ironically, must rely on a moral law known apart from Scripture in exegeting the Scripture that he claims does not affirm the knowledge of the moral law apart from Scripture.

Here's another way to think about it. Imagine someone said to you that the only source for our knowledge of grammar was the Holy Grammar Book. You would think to yourself, "Wait a second. Don't I have to know *grammar* before I read and understand the Holy Grammar Book? And if I do, then it is not true that the Holy Grammar Book is the only source for our knowledge of grammar. For the first person who read the Holy Grammar Book already knew grammar before he read and understood the book." In the same way, the moral attitude with which one should approach any text, including Scripture, is logically prior to reading the text.

Someone could argue that I am offering a hermeneutical principle (i.e., a rule of interpretation) rather than a moral one. But I do not think that is right. For these are not mutually exclusive if one thinks that a proper approach to texts is part of what it means to be a virtuous person. After all, if we discovered that an interpreter of Scripture had been negligent, uncharitable or dishonest in his biblical exegesis, we would not only suspect error in his interpretation, but we would also attribute to him a lack of personal virtue. This judgment would be, at its root, moral.

CONCLUSION

It seems reasonable to believe that there exists a natural moral law, the foundation of just government, and that this natural moral law is best accounted for by the existence of God. Ironically, this seems a better bulwark against the threat of theocracy (which is feared by some unbelievers) than a government whose principles are unstable because they are based on nothing more than power, stipulation or popular sentiments. So, ironically, an atheist is better protected in her rights in a state that is grounded in theism than is a Christian in an atheistic state. Perhaps this is why Dawkins, Hitchens and their atheist colleagues have more political freedom to preach their message in largely Christian America than did Aleksandr Solzhenitsyn and other persecuted Christians in the atheistic regime of the Soviet Union.

CONCLUSION

In this small book we covered five topics essential for introducing politics to a Christian citizen living in a liberal democracy: (1) the study of politics, (2) liberal democracy and the Christian citizen, (3) the separation of church and state, (4) secular liberalism and the neutral state, and (5) God, natural rights and the natural moral law.

In the first chapter I offered an overview of the academic study of politics by briefly introducing the student to six areas of research and interest: political theory, comparative politics, American politics, international relations, political economy and public law. There are many other areas of study, though these six seem to be the ones that overlap many concerns of Christian citizens.

Chapter two explored the nature of liberal democracy and what the Christian faith, including the Bible, can teach us about political principles and what we owe our communities. We also delved into the question of whether or not it is permissible for a Christian to support a non-Christian candidate for public office.

In chapters three through five we examined the relationship between theological beliefs and their role in the lives of citizens and the government in a liberal democracy. In chapter three, we took a look at the always-controversial question of the meaning of the separation of church and state. We assessed its history and how the idea of church-state separation has changed over time, shifting from an emphasis on the relationship between the institutions of church and state to the practices and beliefs of religion and politics.

Because there are some thinkers who argue that liberal democracy either limits or excludes religious voices from shaping public policy, chapter four dealt with secular liberalism, a view that calls for a neutral public square, which in fact turns out to provide unfettered dominance to perspectives that are inconsistent with liberal democracy. Rather than increasing liberty and political engagement, secular liberalism functions as a type of metaphysical litmus test that excludes religious and traditional points of view without even allowing proponents of these views to make their case. Christians should be leery of a perspective, like secular liberalism, that stipulates without argument that political positions that are theologically informed are automatically inferior and thus not worthy of serious consideration in the public square.

The Declaration of Independence (1776) includes these famous words: "We hold these truths to be self-evident, that all men are created equal, that they are endowed by their Creator with certain unalienable Rights, that among these are Life, Liberty and the pursuit of Happiness."[1] In chapter five we answered the question of whether it is reasonable to believe, as the American Founders believed and the Declaration of Independence affirms, that if there exists a natural moral law, the foundation of natural rights, is it best accounted for by the existence of God? Although my answer to that question is yes, we also addressed the issue of whether it is consistent with God's revelation in Scripture that one can have knowledge of a natural moral law apart from that special revelation. I answered yes to that question as well.

Like so much of life on this side of eternity, politics must be put in perspective. It is not everything, but neither is it nothing. It has its place. For this reason, it is the better part of wisdom to end this brief tome with the oft-quoted, but not often reflected on, words from the book of Ecclesiastes:

> For everything there is a season, and a time for every matter under heaven: a time to be born, and a time to die; a time to plant, and a time to pluck up what is planted; a time to kill, and a time to heal; a time to break down, and a time to build up; a time to weep, and a time to laugh;

---

[1]U.S. Declaration of Independence (1776), par. 2.

a time to mourn, and a time to dance; a time to throw away stones, and a time to gather stones together; a time to embrace, and a time to refrain from embracing; a time to seek, and a time to lose; a time to keep, and a time to cast away; a time to tear, and a time to sew; a time to keep silence, and a time to speak; a time to love, and a time to hate; a time for war, and a time for peace. (Eccles 3:1-8 esv)

To be sure, the world of politics is often messy and teeming with conflict. But that's true of so much of life that is worth engaging, whether it's family, church, school or workplace. Thus, it is my hope that the readers of this book will take seriously the wisdom of Ecclesiastes and discern the proper times for their engagement in the world of politics.

Recommended
Contemporary Readings

Although many of the following authors below hold differing views on the relationship between politics, Christianity and the nature of government, they have the virtue of offering well-argued cases for their points of view.

Arkes, Hadley. *First Things: An Inquiry into the First Principles of Morals and Justice.* Princeton, N.J.: Princeton University Press, 1986.

———. *Natural Rights and the Right to Choose.* New York: Cambridge University Press, 2002.

Arnhart, Larry. *Darwinian Conservatism.* Charlottesville, Va.: Imprint Academic, 2005.

———. "Darwinian Conservatism and the New Natural Law." *The Good Society* 12, no. 3 (2003): 14-19.

Audi, Robert. *Religious Commitment and Secular Reason.* New York: Cambridge University Press, 2000.

Audi, Robert, and Nicholas Wolterstorff. *Religion in the Public Square.* Lanham, Md.: Rowman & Littlefield, 1997.

Baker, Hunter. *The End of Secularism.* Wheaton, Ill.: Crossway Books, 2009.

Bauman, Michael, ed. *Man and Marxism: Religion and the Communist Retreat.* Hillsdale, Mich.: Hillsdale College Press, 1991.

———. *Morality and the Marketplace.* Hillsdale, Mich.: Hillsdale College Press, 1994.

Beckwith, Francis J. *Defending Life: A Moral and Legal Case Against*

Abortion Choice. New York: Cambridge University Press, 2007.

Beckwith, Francis J., and Gregory P. Koukl. *Relativism: Feet Firmly Planted in Mid-Air.* Grand Rapids: Baker, 1998.

Boonin, David. *A Defense of Abortion.* New York: Cambridge University Press, 2002.

Bradley, Gerard V. *A Student's Guide to the Study of Law.* Wilmington, Del.: ISI Books, 2006.

Budziszewski, J. *Natural Law for Lawyers.* Nashville: ACW Press, 2006.

———. *True Tolerance: Liberalism and the Necessity of Judgment.* New Brunswick, N.J.: Transaction Books, 1992.

Canavan, Francis A. *The Pluralist Game: Pluralism, Liberalism, and the Moral Conscience.* Lanham, Md.: Rowman & Littlefield, 1995.

Carey, George W. *A Student's Guide to American Political Thought.* Wilmington, Del.: ISI Books, 2005.

Carter, Stephen L. *The Culture of Disbelief: How American Law and Politics Trivialize Religious Devotion.* New York: Anchor Books, 1993.

———. *God's Name in Vain: The Wrongs and Rights of Religion in Politics.* New York: Basic Books, 2000.

Christman, John. *Social and Political Philosophy: A Contemporary Introduction.* New York: Routledge, 2002.

Cromartie, Michael, ed. *Caesar's Coin Revisited: Christians and the Limits of Government.* Grand Rapids: Eerdmans, 1996.

Dreisbach, Daniel L. *Thomas Jefferson and the Wall of Separation Between Church and State.* New York: New York University Press, 2002.

Dworkin, Ronald. *Life's Dominion: An Argument About Abortion, Euthanasia, and Individual Freedom.* New York: Vintage Books, 1993.

Eberle, Christopher. *Religious Conviction in Liberal Politics.* Cambridge: Cambridge University Press, 2002.

Elshtain, Jean Bethke. *Democracy on Trial.* New York: Basic Books, 1995.

Finnis, John. *Natural Law and Natural Rights.* New York: Oxford University Press, 1980.

Galston, William. *Liberal Purposes: Goods, Virtues, and Diversity in the Liberal State*. New York: Cambridge University Press, 1991.

George, Robert P., and Jean Bethke Elshtain, eds. *The Meaning of Marriage: Family, State, Market, and Morals*. Dallas: Spence, 2006.

George, Robert P. *The Clash of Orthodoxies: Law, Religion, and Morality in Crisis*. Wilmington, Del.: ISI Press, 2001.

———. *Making Men Moral: Public Morality and Civil Liberties*. New York: Oxford University Press, 1992.

Grasso, Kenneth L., and Robert P. Hunt, eds. *Catholicism and Religious Freedom: Contemporary Reflections on Vatican II's Declaration on Religious Liberty*. Lanham, Md.: Rowman & Littlefield, 2006.

Gutmann, Amy, and Dennis Thompson. *Democracy and Disagreement*. Cambridge, Mass.: Harvard University Press, 1996.

Hamburger, Philip. *Separation of Church and State*. Cambridge, Mass.: Harvard University Press, 2002.

Hauerwas, Stanley. *After Christendom? How the Church Is to Behave if Freedom, Justice, and a Christian Nation are Bad Ideas*. Nashville: Abingdon, 1991.

———. *In Good Company: The Church as Polis*. Notre Dame, Ind.: University of Notre Dame Press, 1995.

Hays, Richard. *The Moral Vision of the New Testament*. New York: HarperCollins, 1996.

Hittinger, F. Russell. *A Critique of the New Natural Law Theory*. Notre Dame, Ind.: University of Notre Dame Press, 1987.

———. *The First Grace: Rediscovering the Natural Law in a Post-Christian World*. Wilmington, Del.: ISI Books, 2003.

Holloway, Carson. *The Right Darwin? Evolution, Religion, and the Future of Democracy*. Dallas: Spence, 2006.

John Paul II. *Evangelium Vitae: The Gospel of Life*. Boston, Mass.: Pauline Books & Media, 1995.

Johnson, Phillip E. *Reason in the Balance: The Case Against Naturalism in Science, Law and Education*. Downers Grove, Ill.: InterVarsity Press, 1995.

Kramick, Isaac, and R. Lawrence Moore. *The Godless Constitution: The Case Against Religious Correctness*. New York: W. W. Norton, 1996.

Lawler, Peter Augustine, and Robert Martin Schaefer, eds. *American Political Rhetoric: A Reader.* 4th ed. Lanham, Md.: Rowman & Littlefield, 2000.

Linder, Robert D., and Richard V. Pierard. *Twilight of the Saints: Biblical Christianity and Civil Religion in America.* Downers Grove, Ill.: InterVarsity Press, 1978.

Macedo, Stephen. *Diversity and Distrust: Civic Education in a Multicultural Democracy.* Cambridge, Mass.: Harvard University Press, 2000.

————. *Liberal Virtues: Citizenship, Virtue, and Community in Liberal Constitutionalism.* Oxford: Clarendon, 1990.

Machan, Tibor. *Classical Individualism: The Supreme Importance of Each Human Being.* New York: Routledge, 1998.

MacIntyre, Alasdair. *After Virtue.* Notre Dame, Ind.: University of Notre Dame Press, 1981.

Mansfield, Harvey C. *A Student's Guide to Political Philosophy.* Wilmington, Del.: ISI Books, 2000.

Montgomery, John Warwick. *Human Rights and Human Dignity.* Grand Rapids: Zondervan, 1986.

————. *The Law Above the Law: Why the Law Needs Biblical Foundations/How Legal Thought Supports Christian Truth.* Minneapolis: Bethany House, 1975.

Morse, Jennifer Roback. *Love and Economics: Why the Laissez-Faire Family Doesn't Work.* Dallas: Spence, 2001.

Mouw, Richard. *Politics and the Biblical Drama.* Grand Rapids: Baker Books, 1983.

Murray, Charles. *Losing Ground: American Social Policy, 1950-1980.* 10th anniversary edition. New York: Basic Books, 1994.

Murray, John Courtney. *We Hold These Truths: Catholic Reflections on the American Proposition.* Kansas City: Sheed & Ward, 1988.

Neuhaus, Richard John. *The Naked Public Square: Religion and Democracy in America.* Grand Rapids: Eerdmans, 1995.

Niebuhr, Reinhold. *Faith and Politics: A Commentary on Religious, Social and Political Thought in a Technological Age.* Edited by Ronald H. Stone. New York: G. Braziller, 1968.

Noll, Mark A. *One Nation Under God? Christian Faith and Political Action in America.* San Francisco: Harper & Row, 1988.

Novak, Michael. *On Two Wings: Humble Faith and Common Sense at the American Founding.* San Francisco: Encounter Books, 2002.

Olasky, Marvin. *The Tragedy of American Compassion.* Chicago: Regnery, 1992.

Pavlischek, Keith J. *John Courtney Murray and the Dilemma of Religious Toleration.* Kirksville, Mo.: Thomas Jefferson University Press, 1994.

Pavlischek, Keith J., and James W. Skillen. "Political Responsibility and the Use of Force: A Critique of Richard Hays." *Philosophia Christi* 3 (2001): 421-45.

Pojman, Louis P. "A Critique of Contemporary Egalitarianism." *Faith and Philosophy* 8, no. 4 (October, 1991): 481-506.

Ratzinger, Joseph. *Truth and Tolerance.* Translated by Henry Taylor. San Francisco: Ignatius Press, 2004.

———. *Values in a Time of Upheaval.* Translated by Brian McNeil. San Francisco: Ignatius Press, 2006.

Ratzinger, Joseph, and Marcello Pera. *Without Roots: The West, Relativism, Christianity, Islam.* Translated by Michael F. Moore. New York: Basic Books, 2006.

Rawls, John. *Political Liberalism.* Revised edition. New York: Columbia University Press, 1995.

Sandel, Michael. *Democracy's Discontent: America in Search of a Public Philosophy.* Cambridge, Mass.: Harvard University Press, 1996.

———. *Liberalism and the Limits of Justice.* New York: Cambridge University Press, 1982.

Shestack, Jerome J. "The Jurisprudence of Human Rights." In *Human Rights in International Law: Legal and Policy Issues,* 1:69-113. Edited by Theodor Meron. 2 vols. Oxford: Clarendon, 1984.

Simmons, Paul D. "Religious Liberty and Abortion Policy: Casey as 'Catch-22.'" *Journal of Church and State* 42, no. 1 (Winter 2000): 69-88.

———. "Religious Liberty and the Abortion Debate." *Journal of Church and State* 32, no. 3 (Summer 1990): 567-84.

Sweetman, Brendan. *Why Politics Needs Religion: The Place of Religious Arguments in the Public Square.* Downers Grove, Ill.: InterVarsity Press, 2006.

Thomson, Judith Jarvis. "Abortion." *Boston Review* 20, no. 3 (Summer 1995): 11-15.

Wallis, Jim. *God's Politics: Why the Right Gets It Wrong and the Left Doesn't Get It.* San Francisco: HarperCollins, 2005.

Weigel, George. *The Cube and the Cathedral: Europe, America and Politics Without God.* New York: Basic Books, 2005.

West, John G. *Darwin's Conservatives: The Misguided Quest.* Seattle: Discovery Institute Press, 2006.

About the Author

Francis J. Beckwith is Professor of Philosophy and Church-State Studies, and Resident Scholar in the Institute for the Studies of Religion, Baylor University. With his appointment in the philosophy department, he also teaches political science and was the associate director from 2003 to 2007 of the J. M. Dawson Institute of Church-State Studies. He was the 2008-2009 Mary Ann Remick Senior Visiting Fellow in the Center for Ethics and Culture at the University of Notre Dame. A former Madison Research Fellow in the politics department at Princeton University (2002-2003), he is a graduate of Fordham University (Ph.D., philosophy) and the Washington University School of Law, St. Louis (Master of Juridical Studies).

Professor Beckwith is the author or editor of over a dozen books, including *Return to Rome: Confessions of an Evangelical Catholic* (Brazos Press, 2009); *Defending Life: A Moral and Legal Case Against Abortion Choice* (Cambridge University Press, 2007); *To Everyone an Answer: A Case for the Christian Worldview* (InterVarsity Press, 2004); *Law, Darwinism, and Public Education: The Establishment Clause and the Challenge of Intelligent Design* (Rowman & Littlefield, 2003); *Do the Right Things: Readings in Applied Ethics and Social Philosophy*, 2nd ed. (Wadsworth, 2002); and *The Abortion Controversy 25 Years After Roe v. Wade: A Reader*, 2nd ed. (Wadsworth, 1998).

His works have been published in a number of academic journals across a wide range of disciplines, including the *Harvard Journal of Law & Public Policy*; *Journal of Social Philosophy*; *International Philosophical Quarterly*; *Hastings Constitutional Law Quarterly*; *Journal of Medicine & Philosophy*; *Review of Politics*; *American Journal of Jurisprudence*; *Catholic Social Science Review*; *Journal of Medical Ethics*; *Public Affairs Quarterly*; *Notre Dame Journal of Law, Ethics & Public Policy*; *Social Theory & Practice*; *Southern Baptist Journal of Theology*; *Santa Clara Law Review*; *Christian Bioethics*; *Nevada Law Journal*; *Journal of Law & Religion*; and *Philosophia Christi*.

His website is <www.francisbeckwith.com>.

Subject Index